McQUEEN'S MACHINES
The Cars and Bikes of a Hollywood Icon

Matt Stone

Foreword by
Chad McQueen

MOTORBOOKS

First published in 2007 by Motorbooks, an imprint of MBI Publishing Company LLC, Galtier Plaza, Suite 200, 380 Jackson Street, St. Paul, MN 55101 USA

Motorbooks titles are also available at discounts in bulk quantity for industrial or sales-promotional use. For details write to Special Sales Manager at MBI Publishing Company, Galtier Plaza, Suite 200, 380 Jackson Street, St. Paul, MN 55101 USA.

To find out more about our books, join us online at www.motorbooks.com.

Editor: Lindsay Hitch
Cover Design: Tom Heffron
Interior Design: Christopher Fayers

Printed in China

Library of Congress Cataloging-in-Publication Data

Stone, Matthew L., 1958–
  Mcqueen's machines: the cars and bikes of a Hollywood icon / Matt Stone; Foreword by Chad McQueen.
      p. cm.
  Includes index.
  ISBN-13: 978-0-7603-2866-8 (hardbound w/ jacket)
  [1. Vehicles—Miscellanea.] I. McQueen, Steve, 1930–1980. II. Title.
TL146.5.S86 2007
791.4302'8092—dc22
[B]
                              2007018065

On the cover:
Steve McQueen at his Hollywood Hills home in 1963, with his Jaguar XK-SS and one of the more than 200 motorcycles he owned throughout his life. *William Claxton*

On the spine:
McQueen astride a Norton on set during the filming of *Le Mans*. *Chad McQueen collection*

On the frontispiece:
Artist Chris Osborne's impressionistic painting of McQueen as Frank Bullitt, with his trademark 1968 Ford Mustang 390 GT fastback. *Chris Osborne*

On the title pages:
Chad McQueen collection

On the back cover:
Do yourself a favor: pull *Le Mans* out of your DVD collection, and watch it again. The sights and sounds of those Porsche 917s and Ferrari 512s more than hold their own nearly 40 years on. *TAG Heuer*

Opposite: *Chad McQueen collection*

CONTENTS

Chad McQueen collection

FOREWORD

Ever since I was a kid, there were always cars and motorcycles around. Why did my dad have such great taste in cars and a passion for racing? I don't know. But listen to Jimi Hendrix, and you'll ask, "Where did that come from?" It was the same with my dad. Some things are just in you.

He loved all things mechanical. Recall the scene in *The Sand Pebbles* where he's in the ship's engine room, talking to the motor. That wasn't acting. That was just him. When we got home from the motorcycle races every weekend, it wasn't dinnertime. It was time to hose down the bikes, clean the air filters, and tighten all the nuts and bolts. We always put things away clean, tight, and ready to ride the next weekend. *Then* we ate dinner.

Even though he never finished high school, he was motivated to learn about engines, electronics, suspensions, setup, and anything else that made a car or a bike run or go faster. If something was wrong with the car, it wasn't "hey, let's call the auto club." He would troubleshoot things until he figured them out for himself. If we got a flat tire, we got out and fixed it. Dad was way more concerned about having the right caster and camber settings than whether his brake calipers were painted to match the car or how big the subwoofers were, like some of the so-called celebrity car types you see on TV these days.

Cars and bikes were woven not only into our family but into Dad's movies. I was only two years old when *The Great Escape* was made, but some of the stories I've heard about the time they spent in Germany are pretty funny. I didn't see much of the filming of the chase scene in *Bullitt*, but I remember that Mustang, and thinking "Wow, that's pretty cool." I went to Boston for the making of *The Thomas Crown Affair*—I'll never forget that beautiful Ferrari NART Spyder or that fully set up, Corvair-powered dune buggy. I watched Dad drive that buggy on the beach, spraying sand and water everywhere, and man, that looked like fun.

Who could forget *Le Mans*? Dad left for the 1970 race and to begin filming the movie before we got out of school. Mom took us to Europe on the SS *France*. He sent a plane for us upon our arrival at La Harvre, which landed at the course near Solar Village, a compound that was set up by his Solar Productions Company to house the cars, race drivers, crew, and equipment. That first day, when we arrived at La Sarthe, they were shooting near the Indianapolis turn. I couldn't believe my eyes: There were four Ferrari 512s on one side of the circuit and a row of Gulf-liveried Porsche 917s on the other. Lola T70s, Porsche 911s, and a strange blue race car called a Matra. I didn't know what that was at first but later learned it made the most glorious noise—ever. I thought, "This is going to be one bitchin' summer."

My dad wasn't afraid of the risks involved in any type of racing, but he was well aware of them and took it all very seriously. He drove those 917s at racing speeds for weeks on end and once told me "Every day, I thought I was gonna get killed." I arrived late to the Solar compound for lunch one day, and all of a sudden, there was weirdness in the air. I heard there was a crash near the White House complex. I so hoped and prayed it wasn't my dad. About 15 minutes later, he pulled up on his Triumph and said, "Come here. I want you to see what can happen in racing." It was David Piper, one of the pro drivers working on the film. I saw what was left of his Porsche 917, in pieces. I remember seeing a wheel, with its A-arms still attached, sitting out in the cow pasture next to the

Evan Klein

track, a long way from the accident. Thankfully, David survived, but he later lost part of his leg due to an infection stemming from the crash. For a 10-year-old kid, it was pretty mind-blowing.

Look at the cars and motorcycles my dad owned or raced during that 25-year period—from the early 1950s in New York, when he got his first car, through the time he died in 1980—and you'll understand how committed an enthusiast he was. He was heavy into bikes and cars during the 1960s and 1970s—golden eras that will never be repeated. I own two of Dad's cars, plus a bunch of bikes, and they're special, to say the least. I remember riding in the passenger seat of his '69 911S when I was a kid. Now, to have that car and be able to take it out and drive it, well, it just brings you closer. Sometimes, I sit and look at the '58 Porsche Speedster

that he bought new and first went racing in, and I think, "beautiful." I'm lucky to be able to do that.

Some two-dozen books have been written about my dad's life and career. Several mention that he liked cars or rode motorcycles. Bill Nolan did a nice book about his racing life. But none put the whole picture together: the cars and bikes he owned, the ones he worked into his films, and racing on two and four wheels. When Matt Stone came to me with this idea, I knew it was a major part of his story that still needed to be told. I hope you enjoy it.

October 2007

ACKNOWLEDGMENTS

Above all, my thanks to Chad McQueen. This project could not and would not have been possible without him. Chad gave me the approval to do it and the promise of his help. And help he did: names, phone numbers, details, and more than a few remembrances. Chad owns two of his father's most significant cars, as well as several motorcycles, and allowed me to drive and photograph them. He authored the foreword, opened doors, and opened himself up to me whenever I asked. He'll be my bro forever because of it.

Thanks to:

Neile Adams McQueen Toffel, the individual who influenced, guided, and shared Steve McQueen's life more than any other. The first and foremost Mrs. McQueen graciously shared photos, memories, and helpful suggestions, and cleared up a few misstatements and myths along the way. She claims to be "no expert on cars or motorcycles" yet knew quite a bit about her husband's passion for them, and she has been a great supporter of this project. I recommend her book, *My Husband, My Friend*, to all McQueen fans (www.myhusbandmyfriend.com). Thank you, Neile; you're a class act and a half.

Barbara Minty McQueen Brunsvold, who showed us all about her few short years as the third Mrs. Steve McQueen in a wonderful book entitled *Steve McQueen: The Last Mile*. After her career as a Ford model, Barbara had designs on becoming a fashion photographer. She carried her camera everywhere, and from it came many images of McQueen as he'd never been seen before. She allowed me the use of several of them—a most personal gesture, for which I'm indebted.

William F. Nolan, journalist and author of the two books about McQueen referenced in the introduction. Mr. Nolan allowed me the use of any and all material found in both of these books, which included invaluable first-person commentary by McQueen. I cannot thank Bill enough for generously allowing us to use these quotes, which give so much insight into the man.

William Claxton, pop culture photographer extraordinaire. "Clax," as McQueen called him, was the actor's friend and visual biographer. He created some of the most memorable images of Steve ever recorded, and luckily, several of them included his cars and motorcycles. These aren't just photos; they're art and convey the many moods and expressions of Steve McQueen.

Michael Keyser, author, racing photographer, and documentary filmmaker. Michael gave us the book *A French Kiss with Death*, the definitive written and illustrated history of the making of *Le Mans*. He also contributed numerous photos and anecdotes to this project—another unselfish pro, and props to his assistant, Ruth Roberts, who made it all work.

Bud Ekins, McQueen's motorcycle muse, stunt double, racing partner, and friend. Ekins endured being interviewed, lent insight, provided access to photos, and shared great stories about Steve. Because he was *there* when they happened.

Racing legends Mario Andretti and Sir Stirling Moss, for their commentary and insight on Steve McQueen as a racer. Andretti raced against him at Sebring, and Moss was a BMC teammate and coached him in the early 1960s.

Special thanks to the incomparable Dave Friedman, who has been photographing motorsport (and other things) for nearly 50 years. He provided several previously unseen images from McQueen's early racing days and also served as the set photographer for Steve McQueen's two final films, *Tom Horn* and *The Hunter*. What makes anything that comes from Friedman so cool is that he, too, was *there*.

Marshall Terrill, who co-authored the above-noted book with Barbara and contributed to the sidebar about Solar Productions. He also helped with contacts and numerous bits of information. His next book, *Steve McQueen: A Tribute to the King of Cool*, will be released in 2008.

The author at the wheel of McQueen's Jaguar XK-SS on Mulholland Drive, Hollywood. *John Kiewicz*, Motor Trend

Marc Cook, journalist and motorcycle expert. Marc wrote the chapter on McQueen as motorcyclist and racer, and did so to a far higher level of credibility than I could have done myself.

Photographer Evan Klein, who expertly and artistically photographed four of the cars in this book; additionally, John Clinard, Winston Goodfellow, Harry Hurst, Chuck Queener, Nigel Snowdon, Bill Warner, Lynn Wineland, and Jeffrey R. Zwart, whose images grace these pages. Additional photography was provided by MPTV, the Archive, Photofest, and *Sports Illustrated*, and I appreciate the support and professionalism of those entities. An extra acknowledgment to *Werkphoto* in Stuttgart, the Porsche factory's in-house archives service, which supplied many fabulous images from Sebring and Le Mans.

Artist Chris Osborne, who allowed me the use of her rendering of McQueen as Frank Bullitt and his iconic Highland Green 1968 Mustang GT 390, which appears on the frontis. You can purchase copies of this work by contacting her at www.chrisoart.com.

The entire production team at MBI Publishing, including Zack Miller, with whom I've enjoyed a professional relationship for more than 15 years; to the talented, witty, and downright pleasant Lindsay Hitch, who made sense of my ramblings; and to Chris Fayers, who made this pile of photos and illustrations look its best.

David Green, Martin Cribbs, and Samara Schanfeld of Corbis International, who manage the licensing of Steve McQueen's name, image, and estate. Based on their cooperation during this project, McQueen's legacy appears in good hands.

The following car owners: Craig Barrett, Lee Brown, Dave Kunz, Ruth and Kent Perkins, Mike Regalia, Jesse Rodriquez, Anton Singer, Dale Walksler of the Wheels Through Time Museum, and Dick Messer and Leslie Kendall of the Petersen Automotive Museum. Plus, quiet thanks to those who wish to remain anonymous.

Tim Considine, an actor and amateur racer not unlike McQueen; they knew each other through the Hollywood and So Cal racing scenes. Tim contributed photos and stories witnessed firsthand.

Additionally: Richie Clyne, the Imperial Palace Auto Collection; Levi Morgan and Jannelle Grigsby, Bonhams & Butterfields; the Divine Mister Geoffrey Day of Mercedes-Benz Public Affairs; Dr. Bruce Sand; Tony Krivanek; journalist Timothy Barton; Freeman Thomas; Bruce Meyer; Chris Claxton; Sean Kelly; Lindsay Mellor, TAG Heuer; Jennifer Flake, Ford Public Affairs; Darren Wright, www.mcqueenonline.com; and Max Scott, executive director of Boys Republic, to which a portion of this book's royalties will be donated in McQueen's name.

To my family, who no doubt sacrificed something while I was digging up information, sorting photos, grinding out text, or watching a Steve McQueen movie for the umpteenth time.

And finally, to you, for reaching into your wallet and extracting your hard-earned dollars (or well-worn credit card). If you didn't buy this book, I'd have no reason to have written it.

Matt Stone October 2007

INTRODUCTION
Steve McQueen: Movie Star Motorhead

In the 1950s, a group of young actors emerged as postwar Hollywood's first true car guys. They were into automobiles and motorcycles long before it was fashionable or the subject of supposed "reality" television.

The racing bug bit James Dean, and it ultimately cost him his life at a far too young age. Paul Newman was into cars from the beginning of his amazing career too, and his starring in the 1969 film *Winning* launched an impressive racing career as a champion sports car driver and ultimately a CART/Champ Car team owner. A handsome James Garner used to cruise his Mercury around So Cal burger joints in the mid-1950s; he went on to star in John Frankenheimer's *Grand Prix* and also became an accomplished off-road racer.

Then, there was Steven Terrence McQueen.

As an actor and cult hero of intergalactic proportion, Steve McQueen needs no introduction here or anywhere else. From his first bits on Broadway in the 1950s to his well-earned place as one of the world's most popular actors, McQueen's star power lived large. Even now, more than 25 years after his untimely passing on November 7, 1980, his legend is intact, his legacy as relevant as ever. But beyond his status on stage and screen, Steve McQueen was a certifiable motorhead.

He helped build a hot rod before he could legally drive. In the service, he hopped up a tank's engine in the hopes of getting it to go faster. As a young acting student, he rode motorcycles through Greenwich Village. In 1970, he nearly won the 12 Hours of Sebring in a Porsche 908. He raced buggies in Baja, rode motorcycles all over the world, and built entire movies around his love of automobiles and motorsport. McQueen would street race his rare

RACING IS LIFE!

ANYTHING THAT HAPPENS
BEFORE OR AFTER
IS JUST WAITING

Chad McQueen

Jaguar XK-SS through the Hollywood Hills at night, then pack a pickup full of pals and dirt bikes and spend the next day busting trails through the California desert. He entered motorcycle races under the pseudonym "Henry Mushman" so that spectators and the other competitors wouldn't treat him differently from anyone else. Pinstriping pioneer Von

Chad McQueen collection

Dutch, auto upholstery legend Tony Nancy, motorcycle champion Malcolm Smith, and dirt bike racer/stuntman Bud Ekins were among his inner circle.

As McQueen's status as an actor grew, so did the influence he had over the content of his films. He often wove cars and motorcycles into those plotlines—with him at the wheel or gripping the handlebars, of course. In the case of 1971's *Le Mans*, racing was the film's reason for being, so hungry was McQueen to make the most realistic motorsport movie ever.

In my capacity as executive editor of *Motor Trend* and *Motor Trend Classic* magazines, I was doing an article on the 1963 Ferrari 250 Berlinetta Lusso that McQueen's wife, Neile, purchased for him as a 34th birthday present. His son, Chad, joined us for the photo shoot. It was an opportunity for him to get reacquainted with one of his father's cars, which he'd not seen since childhood, and drive it for the first time.

Chad and I were sitting on a curb, admiring the Ferrari's sculpted profile, when he remarked, "That looks like something Dad would have owned. He liked darker, subtle colors. He just had the greatest taste in cars." At that moment, something clicked in my head, and I knew I had to do this book. Steve McQueen had the passion, knowledge, taste, desire, and wherewithal to own a wide variety of impressive and often eclectic machinery.

A few words about what *McQueen's Machines* is not. This isn't a Steve McQueen biography. If you want to study his life, his loves, his many moods, and what he ate for breakfast in endless detail, you'll be disappointed, as there's no Hollywood scandal or tabloid rag stuff here. There are more than 20 McQueen biographies out there from which to choose.

Two to consider are *Steve McQueen: Star on Wheels* and *McQueen*, both by William F. Nolan. Mr. Nolan was one of a few journalists that McQueen confided in and spoke freely with. These volumes contain irreplaceable first-person commentary about cars, motorcycles, and McQueen's racing exploits, and Mr. Nolan has graciously permitted me

Porsche Werkphoto

Motor Trend

photography subject you're interested in, then do not miss *Steve McQueen: William Claxton Photographs*. Several examples from the latter appear in this volume.

McQueen's three wives have written about their lives with him. Neile Adams' book is entitled *My Husband, My Friend*. She was McQueen's first wife, bore his son Chad and daughter Terry, guided his career, and impacted his life more than anyone. They divorced in 1972. Actress Ali MacGraw figures less in McQueen's automotive persona. She dedicated one chapter to her life with Steve in her biography, *Moving Pictures*. They married in 1973 and divorced in 1978.

Cosmo model and McQueen's widow, Barbara Minty McQueen Brunsvold collaborated with Marshall Terrill on *The Last Mile*, a never-before-seen collection of photographs of McQueen, late in his life. She and McQueen spent about two and a half years together, marrying just 10 months before his passing.

Nor is this a filmography, although it is impossible to discuss Steve McQueen's cars, motorcycles, and racing endeavors without getting into certain of his movies. In several instances, they are inextricably interwoven. Take, for example, the iconic car chase sequence in *Bullitt*, still considered the best ever captured on film. It wouldn't be what it is had not Steve McQueen—as actor, filmmaker, car enthusiast, racer, even stunt driver—been involved in all aspects of the scene's makeup. Consider *On Any Sunday*, in which he demonstrated his considerable riding prowess. Nor would dashing business-tycoon-turned-bank-robber Thomas Crown be ripping around a beach in a hopped-up dune buggy in *The Thomas Crown Affair* had not McQueen played him.

This book is about Steve McQueen as a passionate car enthusiast, racer, and motorcyclist. Included are vehicles he owned, those he raced, and others that he drove, rode, or that appeared in his films in other ways. A few qualify under multiple categories. I could not document every machine that passed through his real and metaphorical garages, as some are simply lost to time.

Aside from those he willed to family or gave to friends, many of his cars and motorcycles were sold at an estate auction in Las Vegas in 1984. Another

the opportunity to use it herein. Any place that McQueen is quoted, know that it was sourced from Mr. Nolan's books, unless specifically stated otherwise. Steve's own words give this text credibility and life.

Another read to consider is *Portrait of an American Rebel*, by Marshall Terrill. It was updated and re-released in 2005. If it's McQueen as pop culture

round of McQueen's machines, belonging to third wife Barbara and other private owners, was auctioned in November 2006 in Los Angeles. You will read more about the specifics of these two events.

It's hard to know exactly why McQueen had such a penchant for anything with a motor attached. It was obvious from a very young age and always remained an element of his complex makeup. His passion for racing might be easier to understand . . . First, because he was given a larger than average scoop of talent for controlling an automobile or a motorcycle. Second, and perhaps more importantly, was his innate competitiveness.

In the above-noted Terrill biography, McQueen's longtime friend and martial arts instructor Pat Johnson said, "Steve was the most competitive individual I ever knew; very, very aggressive . . . In karate, you bow to each other before you begin to actually fight. Once we bowed, he would come across the ring at me, I mean both feet, arms, swinging and punching and kicking as hard as he could. Now, I know he loved me like his brother, but that was his nature, this aggressiveness, this competitiveness. But I never knew it to be anything negative."

Bud Ekins, McQueen's motorcycle muse, racing teammate, stunt double, and lifelong pal, put it this way: "He was competitive at anything he did. It didn't matter if it was lagging nickels, riding a horse or a bike, driving a car, whatever. He moved well and was very good physically. He was a good racing driver. Not a great one, I mean, not good enough for Formula 1 or anything, but really good in sports cars. He was an even better dirtbike racer. Hugely talented."

I never met the King of Cool, but by researching this project—through these cars and bikes, through his films, and in speaking with family members and friends—I could feel the heat. I have come to know him in certain ways—the ways that made Steve McQueen pop culture's most legitimate car guy.

Sports Illustrated

Chapter 1

McQUEEN'S GARAGE

To me there are cars, and then there is transportation. I don't have a lot of interest in cars that won't go fast and stop well and corner a little. I'd rather sink my fanny into a bucket seat than park it on a bench. I won't sue if you spread the word that I like to drive flat out whenever the road and the law let me.

—Steve McQueen, *Sports Illustrated*, August 1966

He was born on March 24, 1930, in Beech Grove, Indiana.

Although this quiet Midwestern town is a suburb of Indianapolis, there's no evidence that the young Steve McQueen ever attended the Indy 500 or visited any of the smaller dirt tracks that pepper the state. His mother divorced his father—a daredevil stunt pilot—when Steve was little more than a baby, and he lived with his uncle in Missouri for several years.

At 12, he helped an older pal assemble a hot rod. "It had an Edelbrock manifold" on its compact Ford V8-60 flathead engine, and "could accelerate with a J-2 Allard, which was the going sports car around this time. Our rod didn't handle for beans, but when the engine stayed together that machine had stark acceleration."

McQueen's formative years were tough, to say the least. He never went to school beyond the ninth grade and lived for a while at the Boys Republic reform school in Chino, California. He had his challenges there too, although he always spoke fondly of this institution and supported it generously throughout his adult life.

At the age of 17, he joined the U.S. Marine Corps, and it was there he again exhibited his love of things mechanical. He was assigned to the tank corps.

Chad McQueen collection

"We had this old tank," he said, "and I thought it could be souped up. So a couple of guys and me, we really worked it over, porting and milling the heads, fooling around with the timing and carburetion. Well, on the day we finished, we took it out for a timed run. And the laugh was on us; it didn't go *any* faster."

After his three-year stint in the service and an honorable discharge, McQueen moved to New York. It was there that he acquired the first motorized thing he could call his own, an Indian motorcycle with a sidecar. It was the first of hundreds of street and racing motorcycles he would own. Yet the automobile that Steve McQueen loved first was the sports car that America loved first as well, an MG TC, which he bought in 1952.

Not long after arriving in the Big Apple, he began studying acting. Soon he was performing in small off-Broadway plays, with varying levels of success. A traveling production of *Time Out for Ginger* brought him to Columbus, Ohio, where he found the MG. Between his pay and poker winnings, McQueen saved up $450. But the owner was asking $750.

"I put down $450 . . . and I told the owner I'd send more money from each overnight stop we made. Which I did. It was finally delivered to me in Chicago. That's when I asked for a raise and got booted out of the play. So, I jumped into my MG and drove it all the way back to New York."

The fun but fragile sports car wasn't the ideal machine for the mean streets of Manhattan. "I sold it after three axles broke," he said, "and the spokes kept shredding out of those wire wheels. I decided to stick with cycles for a while." Actor Martin Landau recalled to Chad that among McQueen's many jobs prior to acting, he did a stint as a motorcycle mechanic, working at one time on James Dean's bike.

Things changed a lot for McQueen in 1956. He was by then starring in a major Broadway play and met dancer/actress Neile Adams, who would become his first wife. By the end of that year, the McQueens were making their way to California. And it was there that Steve McQueen's life as a major Hollywood star—as well his passionate relationship with automobiles, motorcycles, and motorsports—began in earnest.

Southern California car culture and Steve McQueen were made for each other. His and Neile's careers were beginning to take off, and successful actors needed cool cars, right? The McQueens had them. In an article for *Sports Illustrated* (see sidebar), McQueen said he "bought an Austin-Healey after I was married, and after that, a Corvette. I shined the Corvette three times and drove it twice while my wife was working in Vegas as dancer. Then, I went back East for a job, and Neile, who was just learning to drive, stuffed the Corvette."

Neile recalls the car and the accident. "One day, he decided it was time to get rid of the Healey and showed up with a Corvette. It was red, and the scallops down the side were white. He left the car with me while he went to St. Louis for a movie. I, having been taught how to drive by my husband, felt really terrific behind the wheel but crashed it rather badly. I took two cars with me in the process. He worked on it so it was drivable and drove it back to L.A. in a very sorry state. We traded it for a new white Ford Fairlane convertible." As McQueen's star began to rise, he bought more, and more interesting, cars.

1953 Siata 208S

Siata was a cottage industry car builder in Turin, Italy. The name that so curiously rhymes with Miata is but an acronym for *Societa Italiana Auto Transformazione Accessori.* Among its (mostly) Fiat-based offspring lies one absolute pearl . . . the 208S Spider.

Fiat tooled up a 2-liter V-8 (dubbed "8V," as according to rumor the Italians thought Henry Ford held a patent on the term "V-8") backed by a four-speed transmission and sold 56 of the driveline packages to Siata. This engine/trans became the basis for the 208S. The overhead-valve V-8 was a curious 70-degree layout and carried an offset pin crank not unlike some modern V-6s. Twin Weber carbs and an unusual distributor with dual points, rotors, and coils added an exotic touch to what could seem like such an American-style engine. The well-finished powerplant put out just over 100 horsepower in Siata trim. Siata backed up the high-tech powerplant with a sophisticated independent suspension design. Rounding out the corners were 400 mm Borrani wire wheels and aluminum drum brakes.

Many enthusiasts caught the sports car bug at the wheel of an MG TC, including McQueen during his early days as a stage actor in New York.
Chad McQueen collection

Covering the simple-but-rigid box section frame was an all-alloy body. As Italian as it certainly is, the package can't help but make you think of a 7/8-size Shelby Cobra 289. The tidy machine rode on a 90-inch wheelbase and tipped the scales at just less than 2,000 pounds. Siata built only 35 of the svelte Spiders in 1952 and 1953.

The 208S was a bit of a boutique sports car, especially on the West Coast. You could buy one from Ernie McAfee Engineering on Sunset Boulevard in Hollywood for $4,995, as McQueen did in 1957 as a replacement for the totaled Corvette. Siatas were raced with some success in Sports Car Club of America (SCCA) events in the late 1950s, and McAfee drove one in the 1953 Mexican Road Race.

A young Dr. Bruce Sand owned Siata 208S chassis number BS 523 right after McQueen, and he recalls meeting up with the actor shortly after he purchased the silver roadster. Sand moved to California to serve his medical internship at UCLA, and he and a friend often cruised by McAfee's place on Sunset.

"I saw the car there and liked it. The guy at McAfee's place told me it was there on consignment from Steve McQueen. He said McQueen had the car a little bit less than a year and was being hassled by his TV studio for racing around in a hot sports car. The price was $4,500."

Sand purchased the Siata and, as he was taking delivery, noticed that the plastic side curtain windows were missing. Someone from McAfee's reached McQueen, who lived nearby. McQueen said, "Send them up."

"He was cordial and seemed to be kind of busy, but he had the parts and gave them to me. I remember distinctly that he had been disassembling his motorcycle on the living room floor, and his wife was yelling at him for getting grease on the carpet. I said thanks and left."

Bruce Sand owned this Siata 208S right after McQueen and drove it on California's storied Pacific Coast Highway about 15 years before the actor moved to Malibu. Here it wears its original silver paint. *Bruce Sand*

McQueen's Siata today, as owned by Everett Singer. *Matt Stone*

About six months later, Sand and his roommate were driving the Siata through the same Hollywood Hills area "and this guy in a Ford convertible comes up alongside and motioned for us to pull over. It was McQueen. We pulled over, and he said, 'I want to drive.' So, my friend got out, and I got in the Siata's passenger seat. McQueen hopped in and took me for one exciting ride. He drove up Coldwater [just north of the Sunset Strip in Hollywood] flat out, really flying. It was getting foggy, and the exhaust note was reverberating through the hills. I thought I was going to die, but much to my surprise, he was so skillful

that the ride was thrilling. He hung a U-turn at Mulholland and headed back toward Sunset. We got back to his car, and he left. He never uttered a word during the entire experience. It was a strange occurrence, to say the least."

Actor turned automotive journalist Tim Considine also remembers McQueen and the Siata. "McQueen was an out-of-work actor from New York when I met him. I hung around Ernie McAfee Engineering practically every day. That's where the Ferraris were, and the OSCAs, and the Morettis, and the Siatas. I lived close, and my roommate worked

One of the cars McQueen is most strongly identified with, his 1958 Porsche Speedster. This photo was taken at Riverside Raceway in 1959; note the racing-style windscreen, rollover hoop, and lack of bumpers. *Chad McQueen collection*

Although it has all the appearance of a 1950s-style chopped top, this is the Speedster's factory-issue removable soft top. The vertical distance from the top of the doorsill to the bottom of the top is only a bit more than the length of a dollar bill. *Evan Klein*

there. McQueen hung out there too. He wasn't famous yet, but since he was an actor who was also into cars, we had something in common."

Considine tells an amusing story about this originally silver sports car and its not-yet-famous owner. "He just loved it. One time he brought the Siata into McAfee's with a problem with the transmission. It was stuck in second gear, as I recall. He had gotten a ticket for going too slow—something like 40 or 45 miles an hour—on the Hollywood Freeway. The guys at Ernie's fixed it, and away he went. My place was just south of Sunset, and my apartment looked out on the street. I heard McQueen drive up and looked out the window. I was just about to yell down to him when Lawrence Tierney [another actor who lived in the neighborhood] came up to the car and they talked, and I heard McQueen say, 'Yeah, it's a Ferrari.' And I thought, 'Oh, really?' He told Tierney that he had gotten a ticket for going something like 150 miles an hour on the freeway. I went back and told my buddies at McAfee's, and we all had a good laugh."

Porsche's iconic Speedster looks particularly good from this angle. Its roundish, organic shape can still be seen in today's Porsches. Along with the Jaguar XK-120 and 140, the MGA, and the Chevrolet Corvette, the Speedster represents what sports cars were all about in the late 1950s. *Evan Klein*

This Siata currently belongs to Everett Anton "Tony" Singer. He was attracted to the model long before it had any connection to the actor. "Back in 1993 and 1994, I was invited to drive in the California Mille with a friend from Florida. During these rallies I saw Barry Silverman's lovely red Siata and was once given a ride. That was it . . . I had to find one. I saw one or two more over the years at various race and concours events, but the time was not right for me until 1999. That summer, I saw BS 523 at Concorso Italiano, where the owner had left an info sheet in the car. I called, negotiated, and finally bought the car in the fall of 2000. The McQueen connection just added to its appeal."

Comparing current and period shots of the car, there have been numerous detail updates and revisions along the way, the most notable being a color change from silver to red when it was restored in the

early 1990s. The rear lighting has been modified along the way and a set of rally clocks added to the instrument panel.

Summarizes Singer: "Its serious show life is over, and I intend on driving the wheels off of it. I am still captivated by its flowing lines, fine handling, wonderful performance, and predictable balance. Each time I see it, I am reminded why I care for it so much and feel lucky to be its caretaker."

1958 Porsche Speedster 1600 Super

The original Porsche Speedster was the perfect Southern California sports car in the 1950s. Its existence was inspired largely by Max Hoffman, Porsche's then U.S. importer. Hoffman wanted a light, inexpensive, roadster version of the 356 devoid

Much of the Speedster's interior and instrument panel is factory original. Note old-style competition seatbelts. *Evan Klein*

The engine bay is neat and tidy without being over-restored. At a rated 75 horsepower, the 1600 Super packed 15 more ponies than the standard 1600 model. McQueen installed an even larger engine after he repurchased the car in 1974. *Evan Klein*

of frills, and the Speedster was it: no rollup windows, no padded top, and wearing a cut-down windshield resembling those fitted to many race cars and American hot rods of the day.

First launched in 1955, the Speedster was intended as a loss leader designed to attract showroom traffic with a low list price. But it became popular for other reasons. The first is that it suited the burgeoning SCCA road racing competition, which was taking hold at the time. And the second is that it appealed to the new, young generation of postwar movie stars in Hollywood. James Dean had one. And so did Steve McQueen.

This black '58 Speedster 1600 Super is significant in so many ways. It was the first car McQueen purchased new. It was the first car he raced in organized motorsports (see Chapter 3). And it is one of three cars he bought, sold, and later repurchased.

Rudge knock-off wheels really set McQueen's Speedster apart. These are a rare and an expensive option, popular for racing, and more often seen on Mercedes 300SLs. *Evan Klein*

Back home again: Bruce Meyer, on the day he delivered McQueen's Speedster back to him in December 1974. "Selling the car back to him was the right thing to do," he says, although Meyer has since purchased an identical car and owns it to this day. McQueen's Mercedes-Benz 300 SEL 6.3 and then-wife Ali MacGraw's 280SE 3.5 convertible can be seen in the background. *Bruce Meyer collection*

Nineteen fifty-eight was officially the last year for the Speedster model (although approximately 30 were built as 1959 models). The standard engine (Normal) was an air-cooled, 1,600-cc pancake four rated at 60 horsepower. But McQueen stepped up a notch to the more powerful Super version, rated at 75. He chose the stealthiest of color combinations—black exterior, black folding top, and a mostly black interior. There wasn't anything on McQueen's Speedster that didn't need to be there, save a small

accessory cigarette lighter clamped to the steering column. One feature that set McQueen's car apart from most others was the optional Rudge alloy knock-off wheels. These were a popular competition accessory, slightly wider than the Speedster's stock steel wheels and a bit lighter too. Perfect for what McQueen intended.

As you'll read more about, McQueen took the car racing and enjoyed early and considerable success with it at several Southern California SCCA meets. He installed an even lower, lighter windscreen, removed the bumpers, and bolted in a roll bar just aft of the driver's seat. It wasn't long before he wanted something faster, more committed. Some say he sold the Porsche in mid- to late 1959 in order to buy a Lotus XI; other sources claim he traded his Speedster directly for the British sports racer. No matter, he owned the Porsche for about a year and a half—at least, the first time around. Los Angeles car collector Bruce Meyer picks up the story.

"In 1965, I was at a local car show. I saw this little black Speedster and fell in love with it. The guy I bought it from said, 'This used to be Steve McQueen's car.' I thought that was cool, although movie star cars weren't as big a deal back then as they are today. I wanted the car and bought it for $1,500. I drove it as my everyday car, suited up in a coat and tie, rain or shine, and had it serviced at Bob Smith Porsche, because I lived in Hollywood at the time. I had owned it for about nine years when Pete [the late Robert E. Petersen, founder of Petersen Publishing Company], who was a friend of McQueen's, told him that he knew the guy—me— who owned his old Speedster. Steve said, 'No way. There's no way he could have that car.'

"A week or so went by, and I got the call: 'Hi Bruce, this is Steve McQueen.' I was trying so hard to be cool. I loved the car, but at that point, I was driving something else every day. He said, 'You've been telling people that this is my car, but that's impossible, because I think that car is long gone. I'd like to see it.' My wife said, 'I have to go with you for that,' and we met in Westwood. He was there before us, and he just broke into a sprint when he saw the Speedster parked on the street. His face just lit up. He said, 'Open the hood,' and there was his old Garner Reynolds racing recap tire. He just went nuts. Then he tore up the carpet behind the seats, and said, 'Yup that's my car! That's where the roll bar was mounted. I gotta have this car.'"

Meyer had no intention of selling and politely told McQueen the same. "For the next two to three months, he called me every week. After a while, I thought, 'If someone offered me one of my favorite cars back, hopefully they would return the favor

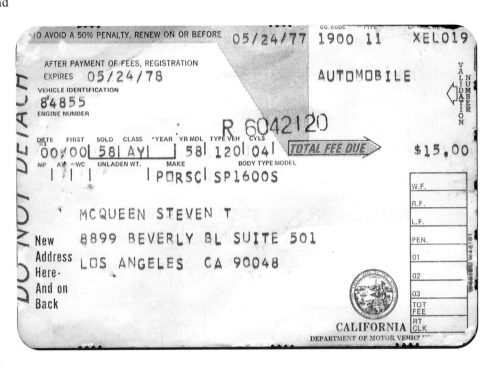

The Speedster's 1977 DMV registration. The Los Angeles address was that of McQueen's business office. *Chad McQueen collection*

some day.' My wife said, 'Don't sell it,' but I told her that if he really wants it and it really means something to him, we should let him have it. So, I sold it to him, in late 1974." By then, McQueen had divorced first wife, Neile, and was married to actress Ali MacGraw, with whom he costarred in 1972's *The Getaway*. "We delivered it to them at their place in Malibu. Even though he was very cool, I felt a little out of my element around him. Ali invited us to stay for dinner, but I didn't feel comfortable about that, and said, 'Naw, we gotta run.' My wife looked at me like, 'Are you crazy? Are you nuts?'"

Upon reacquiring the Speedster, McQueen had some restoration work done, which included re-installation of the bumpers. It's likely he redid the seats, as they have a later, sportier insert pattern resembling a Porsche 904's. Along the way, the car lost its "Speedster" and "Reuter body" fender emblems. One story is that McQueen had removed them the first time he owned the car, preferring the cleaner look, although those badges are in place in photos of the car taken at the races in 1958 and 1959. These trim pieces had already been removed when he bought it back in 1974, so it's hard to say for sure who made this modification and when it took place. McQueen owned the car the rest of his life.

It matters little who jettisoned that "Speedster" lettering, because the Porsche's current owner—Chad—will never put it back on. "Whenever I take it to a car show," he says, "people leave me notes letting me know they have the missing parts if I ever want them. But this is the way Dad liked it, and so there's no way I'm changing it." Chad has gone out of his way to preserve as much of the Speedster's originality as possible. He repainted it and freshened the engine, as the valves were worn. But otherwise, the compact black Porsche is as his father owned it, never having suffered any rust or accident damage.

The 1600 Super engine splutters to life after some cranking with the gas pedal on the floor. It makes familiar, VW-like sounds, but at 75 horse-power has more than double the 36 horses offered in the Beetle of the same era. It feels so sporty: low slung with a wide-open view, thanks to the lack of a top and side windows, and that race-inspired windscreen. The three main gauges are easily visible through the wheel, with the tach top and center. The shifter—a thin, black metal rod, really—sprouts from the floor, as do the pedals.

"Take care of my baby," Chad says as I head out toward California's storied Pacific Coast Highway in Malibu, where his father drove this very machine five decades ago. An open car intensifies any driving experience. I'm ever more aware of the blue sky above, the even bluer Pacific to my left, and how large a Suburban looks from the cockpit of this pint-sized Porsche. The tach suggests that the optimum power band is

from 3,000 to 5,000 rpm, and it is correct. There isn't much power to be had below that, but driven in its sweet spot, the Speedster moves smartly.

What really impresses is how tight the structure is—no rattles or squeaks, and minimal chassis flex for an open-topped car. Everything smacks of quality: the chrome, the gauge faces, the tightly woven beige carpeting, the body seams and gaps. The shifter is long and feels sloppy compared to more modern sports cars, but the ride is better than expected. Push the Speedster through corners, and the tail will happily step out to greet you, and the all-drum brakes are nothing to shout about. But driven deftly, it'll still cover ground in an entertaining way, and it delivers impressive performance for its time. It's easy to understand why Steve McQueen chose this as his first new car and his initial racing weapon.

Will the Speedster ever leave the McQueen family again? Chad smiles a knowing grin. I guess that means no.

1957 Jaguar XK-SS

Jaguar was a dominant force in racing during the 1950s. Ferrari was already a major player, and on the right day, Aston Martin and Maserati got their licks in. Porsche's star was rising, too, but it was Coventry's fast, dependable, and downright beautiful XK-120Ms, C-Types, and D-Types that commanded so many sports car and endurance races. Jaguars won the 24 Hours of Le Mans five times that decade, notching the hat trick in 1955, 1956, and 1957, plus countless other professional and amateur victories in Europe and the United States.

The D-Type was among the definitive front-engine sports racers of the era. It was straightforward yet technologically advanced for the time, powered by Jaguar's already legendary XK dual overhead cam (DOHC) inline-six. Designed during late 1952 and 1953, and raced by the factory team from 1954 to 1956, the D-Type employed a unique chassis layout. Everything aft of the firewall was a monocoque tube; everything forward of it was a tubular structure that held the engine, front suspension, and aluminum front-hinged hood. Its sensual form was the work of

Like his '58 Speedster, this Jaguar XK-SS is one of the cars McQueen is most strongly identified with. And as with the Porsche, he sold it once, only to buy it back later in life. This 1962 photograph was taken at McQueen's Solar Drive home in the Hollywood Hills. *Chad McQueen collection*

Jaguar designer and aerodynamicist Malcolm Sayer and company patriarch William Lyons.

Most factory D-Types were equipped with 3.4-liter XK engines wearing a trio of side-draft two-barrel carburetors and employing dry-sump oiling. The earliest were factory-rated at around 250 horsepower, and the engine was backed by Jaguar's own all-synchro four-speed transmission (not to be confused with the Moss box used in production cars). In total, 67 such D-Types were constructed (plus the factory's own racers), and they competed into the early 1960s. But by the time the factory pulled out of racing after the 1956 season, the car was becoming dated as a front-line racer. Jaguar found itself with 25 customer D-Types on hand—and no customers.

It's not clear who first came up with the idea to convert them to street spec and sell them as limited-edition GTs, but that's what Jaguar did. A full-width windscreen was added up front, and a just-adequate top and luggage rack were grafted onto the rear deck in place of the dorsal fin. Removable fixed-pane side

curtains were mounted to the doors. A vestigial exhaust system was devised, including a shield that only somewhat reduced the number of calves singed on the hot sidepipes. The lighting was converted to street spec, two upholstered seats were installed, a passenger-side door and four corner bumperettes were added, and that was that.

A total of 16 of these XK-SSs were built. At least two were later reconverted to D-Type racing configurations, and a few that were factory-finished as race cars were later transformed into SS spec, or something similar. Only 16 of the 25 remaining cars left the factory before a massive fire struck in February 1957, destroying much of Jaguar's work-in-process inventory—including the final nine D-Type/XK-SSs.

According to Jaguar historian Phil Porter, XK-SS 713 (corresponding to D-Type chassis 569) was originally off-white with a red interior and was imported by Jaguar Cars North America in April 1957. In spite of the left-hand-drive destination, it was a right hooker. Its first owner was building contractor

James Peterson, who lived in Altadena, California, and was involved in the construction of Riverside International Raceway. He soon sold the rare Jaguar to local radio/TV personality Bill Leyden, who often parked it on a studio lot on Sunset Boulevard in Hollywood, where McQueen saw it for the first time. McQueen purchased the car in 1958 for $5,000. "I

know exactly how much we paid for it," recalls wife Neile. "I signed the check!"

McQueen added his imprint to 713. He repainted the exterior a more discreet British Racing Green. Tony Nancy restitched the interior in black leather. Von Dutch fabricated a metal glovebox door to cover the previously open storage space in the dash, purportedly to keep McQueen's shades from flying out of the cubby while he was giving the Jag a thrash. McQueen affectionately nicknamed it the *Green Rat*.

McQueen sold 713 to mega collector William F. Harrah in late 1967, under the premise that it remain on permanent display at his Harrah's Auto Collection in Reno. A decade later, McQueen wanted the car back, and after a two-year negotiation said to be sometimes friendly, sometimes less so, he repurchased it.

In 1984, the XK-SS was sold at McQueen's estate auction to Richard Freshman, McQueen's friend and former neighbor, for $148,000 (another source says $147,500). Freshman commissioned a high-quality yet sympathetic restoration/preservation carried out by Lynx in England. He insisted that McQueen's modifications remain. Freshman sold the special Jag to current owners Margie and the late Robert E. Petersen in 2000, enhancing their collection of movie-star cars.

Mulholland Drive runs along the uppermost ridge of the Hollywood Hills and the eastern portion of the Santa Monica mountains. Depending on where you are on this storied street, you can look to the north to see Warner Brothers, Universal Studios, and the Hollywood sign. Pan south, and seemingly all of Los Angeles, from downtown to the Pacific coastline, lies out in front of you like a giant ant farm. Mulholland is a curvaceous ribbon of pavement that winds up, down, and around for miles.

It's here that McQueen, sometimes with a few pals, would take his cars out to play, usually between midnight and 4 a.m. It took only minutes

The vestigial exhaust system does little to quiet the XK six's bark, although with this car being a right-hand-drive model, the noise exits opposite the driver. The luggage rack is necessary, as there's no cargo space to speak of. *John Kiewicz*, Motor Trend

A classic within a classic: Jaguar's double-overhead-cam XK inline six, which powered the original XK-120 sports car of 1948 and every other Jag produced throughout the 1950s and 1960s. It was good for 250–275 horsepower, which gives an impressive power-to-weight ratio of about one horsepower for every eight pounds, about the same as a C5 Corvette. *John Kiewicz*, Motor Trend

to get from his home on Solar Drive (where he lived from 1960 until mid-1963 and which inspired the name of his film company, Solar Productions—see Chapter 2) to Mulholland.

Fitting my large frame into the XK-SS's compact confines is a chore but worth it. Nancy's neatly patterned leather interior has developed a rich patina and, save minor wear, remains in excellent condition. The wood-and-aluminum steering wheel sits close to the chest, and the large, classic Smiths speedo and tach are just to its left. From this vantage point, you see curves everywhere: the small, tightly wrapped windshield, the roundness of the nose, and most of all, those arching fenders that resemble feline and female body forms.

The starter motor cranks hard against the XK's 12.0:1 compression ratio, but the engine lights with a serious bark out the left flank. Volumes of sounds pour out—a throaty, race-bred gurgle, like that of an expensive motorboat and one that could come only from a straight six. McQueen would hold a cig and drape the steering wheel with his right hand and row the stubby, aluminum-knobbed shifter with his left. First gear is tall—good to over 50—yet second and third are spaced close to keep the growling six on the boil. With around 300 horsepower from the blue-printed XK six on tap, and an estimated weight of little more than 2,000 pounds, the XK-SS isn't quick . . . it's genuinely fast, even in today's terms. Five-second 0-to-60 times were positively exotic for 1957.

Custom leather interior by Tony Nancy has been well preserved. Nancy created stitch patterns based on the size of the seat and other cues in a car's interior, so no two were exactly alike. This was likely the first interior job that the drag racer, hot rodder, and upholsterer crafted for McQueen, but it was by no means the last. *John Kiewicz*, Motor Trend

There's a vintage feel about 713, yet it doesn't seem like a 50-year-old car. I couldn't drive 713 as hard or fast as McQueen did—it's a 2.5 to 3.0 million-dollar piece nowadays—but I couldn't help snapping off crisp 1-2 shifts at about 5,000 revs. Gas it, and the exhaust note hardens to a throaty blare, harmonized by a reedy intake noise from the sidedraft Webers. The pipes pop and spit when you let off the gas. Heat waves boil out of the hood vents. Intoxicating.

Local legend holds that at least one L.A. law-enforcement agency had promised an expensive steak dinner to the officer who could nail McQueen and the Jag with a speeding ticket. The tale continues that, while he was spotted often and even pursued a time or two, he was never caught and the ticket never written. The steak dinner went unclaimed. Another story refutes the entire affair, alleging that McQueen was so awash in speeding tickets he nearly lost his license.

Hooray for Hollywood.

1963 Ferrari 250 Lusso

It's common knowledge that Enzo Ferrari constructed road cars only as a means to support his company's racing activities. The street machines hit their stride with the advent of the 3.0-liter 250 series cars in the late 1950s. The original Testa Rossa, the 250 Short-Wheelbase Berlinetta (SWB), *continued on page 39*

Yesterday and Today: Steve McQueen (above) on his way to Carmel, California, at the wheel of his new Ferrari Lusso in 1963.
Chad McQueen (below) piloting the same car for a magazine photo shoot, Los Angeles, California, 2005. *William Claxton, Evan Klein*

The Lusso's connection to the GTO, which was really more of a race car than a grand tourer, is clear. McQueen had already done a fair share of racing by then, and while it is believed he took the Lusso for a few laps around Riverside International Raceway, he used it primarily for long, fast road trips and cruising around L.A. *Evan Klein*

Clowning for Clax: Peggy Moffitt, model and wife of photographer William Claxton, and McQueen ham it up for the camera, replete with a champagne toast, for a *Cosmopolitan* magazine spread in 1964. McQueen must have liked how he looked as a wealthy man, as it isn't so different from Thomas Crown, whom he played a few years later. *William Claxton*

While Ferrari's road-going version of the Colombo-series 3.0-liter V-12 wasn't the most powerful street engine the company ever made, it was among the sweetest. It was tough, was tractable at lower rpm, and made that trademark "silk being ripped" sound at high revs. In three-carb Lusso form, it was rated at 250 horsepower. *Evan Klein*

continued from page 35
and the seminal 250 GTO were racing icons of the era. The 250 GT coupe and cabriolet, California Spyder, and GTE 2+2 models bolstered the marque's growing roster of exotic street machines.

Yet the final example of this 250 Grand Touring species, the Lusso, is considered by many Ferrari lovers the most sensual and seductive. Some 350 examples (excluding a couple of prototypes) were produced in 1963 and 1964, although the first production version made its debut at the Paris Salon in 1962. Most striking is the voluptuous body sculpture designed by Pininfarina, and rendered in steel and aluminum by Scaglietti.

Genealogically, the Berlinetta Lusso is first cousin to the 250 GT/SWB and GTO, sharing the same basic tubular chassis design and V-12 engine configuration. Power for the Lusso comes from a detuned version of the Colombo-designed 60-degree V-12 used in both the GT/SWB and the GTO, featuring single overhead cams and a 9.01:1 compression

ratio. If used for racing, this engine would carry six— but the Lusso sports only three—36-DCS Weber twin-choke downdraft carburetors. In street trim, the package produces approximately 250 horsepower, with a top speed approaching 150 miles per hour.

As a precursor to Steve's 34th birthday in March 1964, Neile bought a Ferrari 250 GT Berlinetta Lusso, serial number 4891, from Otto Zipper Motors in Santa Monica, California, via Luigi Chinetti in New York. Chinetti was the North American importer of Ferraris, and Mrs. McQueen recalls paying $14,000 for the car. It was ordered in a medium-brown metallic hue called Marrone, with a beige interior— an odd, yet elegant, color combination.

The Lusso quickly became a favorite for high-speed road trips. Noted pop-culture photographer William Claxton, a close friend of McQueen's, relates a trip taken a week or so after the actor got his Ferrari. According to Claxton, the McQueens invited Claxton and his wife, Peggy, on a getaway. Their route took them from Los Angeles to Big Sur,

Carmel, Monterey, then through San Francisco, Reno, Lake Tahoe, Death Valley, and back to Southern California.

Said Claxton: "We would set a place to meet for lunch and then take off, Steve in the Lusso and me in my Porsche 356 SC 1600. Steve's idea of fun was to go roaring off and, a couple hours later, be parked at the side of the road pretending to be bored waiting for us to arrive. It was a great time. He really loved that car."

The love affair with the Lusso lasted for several years. However, a constant irritation developed concerning its propensity for burning oil and smoking under hard acceleration. The cause of the problem was soft, easily worn valve guides. McQueen had the car's engine rebuilt, but the oil smoke persisted.

The affair waned, and he is believed to have sold the car in 1967.

Number 4891's post-McQueen history is largely known, save for a few murky spots. In July 1973, an ad appeared in *Competition Press & Autoweek*, offering the Lusso for $12,900. In 1974, San Francisco collector Tom Sherwood purchased it. He was a low-key owner, keeping the car and enjoying it for occasional drives. During his 20-plus years of ownership, Sherwood clocked about 6,000 miles.

In late 1997, Sherwood sold the car to Mike Regalia, a respected restoration expert and, for many years, president of the famed Nethercutt Collection of automobiles and mechanical instruments. In an odd twist, the deal between Sherwood and Regalia included a rare, handmade, black-powder 45-caliber

It's the slim roof pillars and elegant greenhouse that give the Lusso not only its fabulous exterior lines but also an airy feel inside. Wire wheels, unobtrusive bumperettes, and an eggcrate grille add to its early 1960s ambiance. An all-time great Ferrari—even in Marrone.
Evan Klein

One of the cars McQueen drove in his road test with *Sports Illustrated* (see sidebar) was a Ferrari 275 GTS. It had a more developed chassis and a bigger engine than his 3.0-liter Lusso, perhaps prompting him to opt for this nearly identical example. There are few photos of this car, and Chad recalls that it was a burgundy color, but its current whereabouts are not known. Here, McQueen cuddles with a go-go-booted Neile at their home in Brentwood, not inappropriately nicknamed "The Castle." *Kurt Gunther/ MPTV.net*

pistol created by Von Dutch, who performed the above-noted fabrication work on McQueen's Jaguar.

The Lusso was in good shape, and Regalia drove it regularly, but, after learning of its history, he felt it deserved a from-scratch restoration, which began in earnest in 2001. The car was gutted and the body stripped of paint down to the bare metal. Regalia, a skilled restoration craftsman, managed the task of refurbishing the coachwork, which is a combination of a steel roof and fenders with aluminum doors, hood, and trunk lid. Regalia reworked all the metal with files and countless hours of hand finishing. With the help of friend Tom Ryan, he repainted the body the appropriate shade of Marrone.

"I struggled with that," recalls Regalia, "because I really don't like brown. But I knew I was a custodian of history, so nothing but the original color would do. I mixed and remixed and tested it several times, being careful not to infuse too much metallic into it."

While the V-12 was out being serviced, the engine compartment was detailed, and all the hardware—every nut, bolt, bracket, and fastener—was plated in the correct finish and reinstalled. All the glass is original, and those beautiful Borranis were rebuilt with new spokes, center hubs, and fresh Dunlop SP Sport-185/15 tires. The car carries its original leather-bound owner's manuals and a period list of Ferrari dealerships, while the unrestored tool kit completes the trunk.

Chad was just over three years old when his father acquired the Lusso. "I don't remember much about it from back then, but I've heard my mom talk about it a lot. It's just beautiful." He drove the car for our photos and was tentative with it at first, but the rising shift points meant he was getting comfy. "It makes a fantastic noise, and once you get some speed, the steering lightens up. It's warm inside, and it sure smells good. That's the original license plate that was on it when my dad had it. As life goes on, I'm getting to drive so many of Pop's significant cars, which is bitchin'. The Lusso feels like something he would have."

1967 Mini Cooper S

As a transportation icon, the mighty Mini rates up there with the Volkswagen Beetle, the Ford Model T, and the Citroën 2CV. If the Beetle was Germany's people's car, the Mini filled the same shoes for England. Launched in 1959, the Mini was a groundbreak-

ing automobile in several senses. It was front-wheel drive, which wasn't yet common for subcompact cars. It used a unique rubber-coned suspension. And its packaging—teensy on the outside, larger inside than expected—was revolutionary.

The terminally cute Mini's main reason for being was cheap, dependable, subcompact transportation. But it didn't take long for the Mini to catch on as a hip fashion accessory. The Beatles drove them. Actors like Peter Sellers and models, such as Twiggy, had them. A fervent aftermarket

continued on page 46

McQueen's smallest four-wheeled machine was this 1967 Mini Cooper S. This photo was taken at Lee Brown's custom paint and body shop in Hollywood, when the happy new owner came to pick it up after a color change and trick touches. Brown says the unconventional single driving light "was strictly McQueen's idea." *Lee Brown*

STEVE McQUEEN, MAGAZINE ROAD TESTER

It isn't unusual for magazines to engage guest authors to participate in or write feature stories. But *Sports Illustrated* pulled off a coup by snaring Steve McQueen to evaluate a group of sports cars for its August 8, 1966, issue. This was a strange time for McQueen as an enthusiast, because his film career was extremely busy, and he wasn't doing much, if any, racing. So it was nice to see him doing what he loved to do—fling cars around a racetrack.

That track was the legendary Riverside International Raceway, about an hour east of Los Angeles. Riverside was an interesting, fast, and technical course, and had been the site of many important races since its construction in the late 1950s. McQueen had raced there in his Porsche Speedster and also tested a Chevy V-8-powered Lola T70 sports racer—a torridly fast machine—so he knew his way through Riverside's famed "Esses" and its infamous, high-speed Turn 9.

The *SI* edit team put together a fabulous group of sports cars for McQueen to play with: Jaguar's new E-Type 2+2, a Mercedes-Benz 230SL roadster, an Aston Martin DB6, an Alfa Romeo Duetto (like his future costar Dustin Hoffman had driven in *The Graduate*), a Porsche 911 (relatively new at the time, as Porsche only began importing them here as 1965 models), a 427-ci big-block Corvette coupe, a Ferrari 275 GTS, and a Shelby 427 Cobra.

McQueen wrote the story in first person, assisted by journalist Ken Rudeen. The main title was "A Star Among Fast Friends" with McQueen's commentary entitled "I Still Get Goose Pimples." Prior to his assessment of each car, McQueen talked about himself as an enthusiast, the first few cars that he owned, and then in more detail about his Jaguar XK-SS and Ferrari 250 Lusso. Of the task at hand, he said, "Understand that I am an actor, not a racing

Neile Adams

PHOTOGRAPHS BY JAMES DRAKE

A STAR AMONG FAST FRIENDS

Steve McQueen is somewhat better known as a movie actor ("The Great Escape," "Nevada Smith") than as a driver of fast cars. But as he demonstrates at right, cornering smartly in the new Jaguar 2+2, and as he says in the story beginning on page 39, he "ain't a bad driver, either." Formerly a sports car racer of promise, McQueen was ordered off the tracks by his studio, on the theory his beautifully battered face needs no further corrugations. He has not lost his enthusiasm for swift motoring, however, and when Sports Illustrated asked him to drive eight of the world's most distinguished Grand Touring cars on the race course at Riverside, Calif., he was, as they say, flat out. Turn the pages for pictures of Steve in a real-life role, and for his analysis of the state of the Grand Touring art in this midsummer 1966.

James Drake, courtesy Sports Illustrated

James Drake, courtesy Sports Illustrated

driver or an automotive engineer, but I've raced some, and I ain't a bad driver. The cars you see in these pages are my kind of automobile. They go and they stop and they handle. They are driver's cars, and most of them have been developed from racing cars. It was a kick driving them around Riverside." Here's a selection of his comments from each:

Ferrari—"With more inches than mine [the Lusso] and a better power arc from its six Weber carburetors—mine has three—I was pushing 140 mph. Top speed in ideal conditions is better than 150. The car was set up just the way I like it—for oversteer in tight corners and understeer in fast ones. . . . The steering was heavy at 20 mph, as it should have been, and became progressively lighter as I went faster. . . . Clicking through the five-speed gearbox was a pleasure; Ferrari gearboxes shift like a knife through butter. You throw the stick, and it just kind of finds its own way."

Alfa Romeo—". . . as I expected, it was marvelous to drive within its limitations. On the narrow, mountainous roads of Italy it would be perfect. The five-speed gearbox was quite good, and I must say I was very impressed by the brakes. I stopped six or seven times from 90 mph and had absolutely no brake fade or locking. Going through Turn One in fourth gear at the rpm limit of 7,000, which is close to a speed of 90, I could not break the rear end loose."

Mercedes-Benz—"The Mercedes 230SL was very handsome, and it sure did handle well. But I thought it was underpowered for the money. The model I drove had the Mercedes automatic transmission. It was the best from Europe that I have come across, but if I were buying the car, I would take the four-speed manual. To be fair about this automatic, it shifted quite accurately, and there was no slugging or mushing. This Mercedes is an outstanding lady's car, yet it will also take some manhandling."

Porsche—"I was curious to see how much the Porsche had changed since I raced my Super, which had the four-cylinder engine. Boy, it's changed. Road noise used to be a problem with that rear-engine location, but on the 911 I got very little noise. . . . The 911 was a very neutral-handling car, very docile, very pleasant to drive, and the five-speed gearbox sure was easy to use. Once a gust of wind caught me on the back straight and slid me over a few feet, but the car didn't get radical in its handling."

Jaguar—"After driving the 2+2 with the automatic transmission, I felt that if you really wanted to get on it, a manual box would be a must in this car. I thought the transmission was sluggish. . . . I had driven the two-seater XKE and, as far as I could see, the 2+2 handled just like it, which is bloody good. I found it very smooth down the back straight at 110 mph. The seat was fine; the visibility was good; the brakes were solid. There is great appeal in the 2+2 for the man who will accept a compromise. He can put his two kids in the back, run his wife in the front and take off for his vacation.

Aston Martin—"The Aston is not a light car, by any means, but the brakes were quite good; there was slight fade after some exceptionally hard use. But, shifting up from fourth to fifth at top revs, you seemed to lose all your beans, lose your power. Both Jaguar and Aston may have to go to more cylinders some day to stay competitive [which they both did within a few

years]. Nowadays the American market is putting out V-8 blocks that are able to pull 400 to 425 horsepower. Those long-stroke English sixes are beginning to be just a little old fashioned by comparison."

Corvette—"I was very impressed by the Corvette. Other than the Ferrari, it was the best car I drove at Riverside. And let's face it, it went out the door at $5,500 instead of $14,000. . . . It must be one of the fastest production cars you can buy for that kind of money. At Riverside, somebody turned on a sprinkler that got some water on the track, and as I was going into Turn One doing 120, I hit it. I kind of got on tippytoes when I hit the water, lifted everything and tippytoed through it, and then I got back on it right away to clear off the tires. No problem. No panic."

Cobra—"The Cobra I enjoyed very much for its acceleration, which is brutal, and its brakes, which really get you stopped. I could not get a realistic idea of how well this particular car can corner, because the gas would slosh to one side of the carburetor bowl and starve out the engine. I know the work Carroll Shelby has put into the car, and I realize that the ones he prepares for racing are set up just right, so I'm reluctant to call myself an expert on it. But it was a real stoplight bandit on acceleration. I understand the 427 can get up to 100 mph and get stopped in just over 13 seconds. That is motoring. And motoring is kind of a good part of life."

James Drake, courtesy Sports Illustrated

Other than a repaint (to not quite the same colors Brown originally sprayed it in 1967), the Mini is as it was four decades ago. The wheels are the stock units, reversed for a wider track. Holes in the fenders indicate that it wore a set of bolt-on flares at some point, although they've since been removed. *Matt Stone*

continued from page 42
sprung up to customize and rebody Minis into all sorts of flavors: wood bodies, convertibles, some trimmed out like a Rolls-Royce inside.

Given its light weight, good handling, and easily modified engine, the Mini caught British racer and car builder John Cooper's attention as a potential performance car. How his ideas ultimately resulted in the development of the Mini Cooper is an interesting story and occupies several volumes. The result had so much impact that today's current Mini models are still dubbed the Mini Cooper and Mini Cooper S.

The first Minis were equipped with 848-cc inline fours, mounted transversely, and rated at just 34 horsepower. The range of Cooper models carried a variety of larger British Motor Corporation fours, with displacements of 970, 977, 978, and 1,071 ccs, all with more power, but the top-of-the-line Mini Cooper S employed a 1,275-cc four. Twin carburetors, bigger brakes, larger wheels and tires, a stiffer tuned suspension, and a host of other mods made the Cooper S a terror for its size.

Cooper correctly judged the Mini's potential on the racetrack. It was a capable stock and modified class competitor in all manner of sports car racing and proved particularly adept in the world rally championship. Race-modified Minis won the prestigious Monte Carlo rally outright in 1964, 1965, and 1967, beating many larger and faster cars in the process. As testimony to its longevity and basic goodness as an automobile, the original Mini remained in production, albeit with consistent updating, from 1959 through 2000—a remarkable 41-year run.

We don't know for sure why Steve McQueen wanted a Mini, but one possible reason may have been his personal association with Cooper. He and McQueen got to know each when the actor was in Britain filming *The War Lover*. Cooper sold McQueen one of his Cooper Formula Junior open-wheel racers in late 1961. He later extended McQueen an opportunity to join the factory Cooper racing team (see Chapter 3).

Lee Brown, who first met McQueen when he came to Brown's Hollywood paint and body shop with his Ferrari Lusso, became involved with the actor's Mini Cooper S. Little did Brown suspect he would end up owning the car a decade after McQueen's passing.

'67 AUSTIN MINI Cooper S owned by Steve Mc Queen (nol867) Evns. Pp

94 ★ Sun., May 20, 1990
Los Angeles Times

"Back in the '60s, if you didn't have a Ferrari and a Mini Cooper, you just weren't a movie star. Well, Steve McQueen already had his Ferrari Lusso and spotted this Mini over at Hollywood Sports Cars." The exact date isn't clear, but it was likely that he purchased the car in early 1967. "He called me up and said, 'I bought it. Go over and pick it up, and I'll come to the shop and we'll figure out what to do with it.' McQueen always did things to his cars to make them his own, and he had certain things that he liked and didn't. The Mini was originally green with a white top, but Steve liked browns and grays and other subtle colors. So we painted it a medium brown metallic with a beige top. It's been repainted since, and the current colors aren't exact. He wanted a wood dash, so we did that, and I also installed the single fog light and the sunken radio antenna."

Brown recalls that Tony Nancy stitched up the interior, although Brown chided McQueen that the mottled, grainy vinyl he selected "looked like it belonged in a booth at a diner" more than in the cabin of a British sports car. Brown installed the large vinyl sunroof when he originally painted the Mini.

McQueen couldn't wait to take his new toy for a ride. "He was really on the button, redlining the car in every gear. We were heading down Franklin Avenue in Hollywood, and at the last instant, Steve decided to make a right turn up one of the canyon roads. He got off the gas and pitched the car around the turn but caught the curb with the right rear tire. That put the car up on the two driver's side wheels. We must have gone that way for 150 feet, McQueen working the wheel to keep us from rolling over or hitting any of the parked cars on the opposite side of the street. Finally, it landed right-side up, on its wheels. We were both white as sheets, and our knees were knocking." The damage to the right rear wheel and tire were minimal, but they very nearly ran out of gas heading home. "Steve was so hot to take the car for a run, neither of us checked the gauge. McQueen, as was often the case, didn't have a dime on him. I had to pay for gas to get us back to the shop."

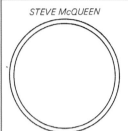

STEVE McQUEEN

November 27, 1967

Mr. Lee Brown
Precision Auto Body
5640 Hollywood Blvd.
Hollywood, California

Dear Lee:

Just a note to let you know how pleased I was
with the work you did on the Mini.

You're the best, man, you really are.

Regards,

Steve

Steve McQueen

Little is known about this mid-1960s Corvette Sting Ray coupe. A young Chad appears in front of it with his maternal grandmother at the McQueen's Brentwood home. This is not the 'Vette that Neile crashed early in their marriage. Its serial number and current whereabouts are unknown. *Neile Adams*

Letter from McQueen to Brown on personalized Solar Productions letterhead.

Brown recounts another amusing story: "I arrived at my shop one morning, and McQueen was there with the Mini. He was agitated and clearly hadn't slept. I asked what was the matter, and he pointed to a big dent on the front fender. He was heading home the previous night and was driving on Mulholland Drive. The area wasn't all that populated back then. He needed to take a leak, so he pulled over to the side of the road. While he was relieving himself, he saw the car roll by him. It was parked on a bit of a grade, he forgot to set the parking brake and must have left the gearshift in neutral too. He went chasing after it, but couldn't catch it in time, and it smashed into a parked car's bumper. He knocked on the peoples' door, and you can imagine their surprise at having Steve McQueen show up on your doorstep in the middle of the night. McQueen said, 'I offered to pay for the damage, but the guy didn't want any money. He said he wasn't going to call the police either, but he just wanted to talk. We sat and talked, and he kept me up until 6:00 in the morning. I practically had to run out of there.' McQueen

came directly to my shop to leave the car off for repair, and it was no wonder he looked so tired."

After a few years, McQueen sold the car back to Hollywood Sports Cars. It was subsequently resold a time or two before Brown spotted it for sale in the classified ads in 1990, approximately two decades after McQueen last owned it. "I verified that it was Steve's car; the guy was asking $10,000, which was a ton of money for a run down Mini." It is in original, unrestored condition, although it hasn't run in years. Even though Lee Brown is more than capable of restoring it, he seems happy to enjoy it just the way it is.

1967 Ferrari 275 GTS/4 NART Spyder

There are Ferraris, and then there are *Ferraris*. The NART Spyder is among the latter—something special even among all the special automobiles from the house that Enzo built.

The original 275 GTB coupe was launched as a 1964 model. It was a departure from the myriad 250-series Ferraris that had been popular for the previous seven to eight years, in that it was powered by a larger engine family (3.3 versus 3.0 liters). There were a number of 275 GTB variants: Long and short nose, steel and alloy bodies, and three series of competition models. A DOHC engine came along in 1966. But in spite of the many varieties of this handsome and versatile Ferrari, all were coupes. Luigi Chinetti changed that for 10 lucky *tifosi*.

Chinetti was Ferrari's North American importer at the time, and NART stood for North American Racing Team, of which Chinetti was principal. Chinetti also drove a Ferrari to victory at the 24 Hours of Le Mans in 1949, Ferrari's first big win as a then fledgling carmaker. All in all, the Chinetti family had the ear and the trust of Enzo Ferrari, something few people could claim.

It was Chinetti's son, Luigi Jr., who had the idea to produce a convertible version of the 275 GTB for NART's American customers. It made sense: convertibles were, and remain, popular here due to good weather, especially along the thousands of miles of U.S. coastline. Sergio Scaglietti, Ferrari's body panel and assembly supplier, redesigned the 275 GTB into a convertible form, and the 275 GTS/4 NART Spyder was born. All had the later 330-horsepower, four-cam V-12 (hence the addition of a "4" to the model name); they were initially sold to North American customers, and just 10 were built.

Steve McQueen first encountered the NART Spyder model during the filming of *The Thomas Crown Affair* in 1967 (see Chapter 2). McQueen as Crown didn't drive the car in the film, as it belonged to Faye Dunaway's character. That particular car, chassis number 09437, was the first NART constructed, and it appeared in the film in two separate scenes. Its total time on screen was about 30 seconds. But it was enough to make an impression on McQueen.

He put in an order with Chinetti and purchased 275 GTS/4 NART Spyder chassis number 10453. It was the sixth in the series of 10, wearing standard steel bodywork (the *Thomas Crown* NART is one of only two that have aluminum coachwork). He took delivery of the car in the spring of 1967.

Auto body craftsman and custom painter Lee Brown, who had previously worked on McQueen's Mini Cooper, picks up the story: "Steve was away at the time. He called me up and said that his new Ferrari was at LAX and that I should go and pick it up. Talk about a driver; what a joy." Brown brought the car back to his shop, awaiting its new owner's inspection.

When McQueen looked it over, the first thing he said was "Gotta paint it. Not my kind of blue." "Imagine that!" recalls Brown. "He spends about fifteen grand on this fabulous new Ferrari, and the first thing he wants to do is tear it apart and change it. But that was McQueen. He knew what he wanted. He'd listen to what other people suggested, consider all their advice, and then do it his way. And he was usually right."

As long as the car was going to be stripped, McQueen told Brown he wanted to "make it neat. Do some stuff to it." Brown recommended that they remove the bumpers to further clean up the look. And since it was a racy car to begin with, Brown suggested an aluminum, quick-fill gas cap. They also agreed on a small, rally-style rearview mirror

Above and opposite: There are but 10 Ferrari 275 GTS/4 NART Spyders in the world, and McQueen crossed paths with two of them. This is the car he owned; the other was the deep red example used in the filming of *The Thomas Crown Affair*. The custom touches on McQueen's NART are easy to spot: more aggressive rear spoiler, racing-style flip-open gas cap, nonfactory blue finish. McQueen owned it only a short while, as it was nearly totaled when he was rear-ended on the Pacific Coast Highway in California. Simply put, one of the world's most desirable Ferrari models. It's more-than-celebrity ownership is just a bonus. *Chuck Queener*

for the driver side. The Ferrari came from the factory with no radio, but McQueen wanted one, so Brown built a small console to hold it. "Steve hated radio antennas, or anything else that cluttered up the lines of a car, for that matter. So I designed a power antenna that fit inside the fenderwell." It was fabricated and installed in such a way that the top of the antenna sat flush with the bodywork. All you could see was the small, circular gap where the antenna knob retracted back to the level of the fender. A sanitary-looking, custom touch, just as McQueen liked. Brown recalls that McQueen's upholsterer of choice, Tony Nancy, came and picked up the seats, redoing them in leather with a different stitch pattern than the factory's.

When the car was done, McQueen came to the shop to pick it up but wasn't pleased with the carefully chosen color. He and Brown got into a "discussion" about it, to no particular resolve. As McQueen left,

Brown told him to be careful with this now even more unique Ferrari and not to "fuck it up." "I think that was on a Thursday. Not more than a few days later—that weekend as I recall—he was out on the Pacific Coast Highway, stopped in light traffic. There were a couple of young gals in bikinis walking down the street, and they caught the attention of two servicemen in a truck that was behind McQueen."

The truck's driver was watching the scenery and not the road ahead. He plowed headlong into McQueen, who was stopped at a signal, smashing up the rear end and pushing the Ferrari into the car ahead of him. According to Ferrari expert Marcel Massini, "It had been hit so hard that both doors were buckled outward; there wasn't an undamaged panel on the car." The hapless Ferrari was stored at a gas station in nearby Pacific Palisades, and as McQueen and Brown had previously argued over the color of the custom paint job, it was taken to another painter,

Junior Conway, to be redone. The NART currently wears a slightly exaggerated rear lip spoiler, and Brown recalls that this bit of custom work was performed while Conway was rebuilding the car.

McQueen sold the car in 1971 to a Southern California Ferrari enthusiast. It was then on the market at a Long Island exotic car dealership and was purchased by its current owner in 1986. Ferrari NART Spyder number 10453 now resides in New York. "I bought it because I really liked it," the owner states. "The McQueen ownership was just a bonus." Yes, it was.

Chevy-Powered Jeep CJ

Biographer Nolan tells an interesting story about McQueen's highly modified Jeep that transpired as the journalist was on his way to meet him for an interview. "I motored upward a mile or two, eased around a long looping curve to find McQueen, unsmiling, looking wary (not trusting me yet), his arms folded across his tanned, shirtless chest, leaning against his Jeep, waiting for me. No ordinary vehicle, this Jeep. Custom paint job. Foam-padded rollbars. Tooled leather bucket seats. Oversized wheels. 'Park your car here, and we'll take this up top where nobody can hassle us.' McQueen slid behind the wheel of his Jeep, and I climbed into the seat next to him as he gunned the engine to thunderous life.

"What have you got under there,' I shouted, pointing toward the hood. 'Five-fifty Traco Chevy. Full race suspension. Light chassis. She can step.' And she did. McQueen's boot on the accelerator sent the 550-horsepower vehicle forward in a raw surge of power that snapped my head back." Indeed a far cry from the overhead-valve four or Buick-sourced V-6 that originally powered this mid-1960s sport/utility. Nolan continued: "McQueen was in a class by himself as he blasted the powerhouse Jeep around each

Blue skies, blue eyes, and a one-of-a-kind Chevy V-8-powered Jeep CJ. Photographer Milton Greene traveled with McQueen to Mexico on a recon trip, in advance of his run in the 1969 Baja 500. This is just one of many fabulous images he returned with. Note the chrome roll bars and wheels, high-back leather Solar Engineering bucket seats, bumper-mounted driving lights, and Von Dutch pinstriping over the tan paint job. Whoever has it owns one of the world's most significant Jeeps. *Milton H. Greene, copyright 2007. Joshua Greene, archiveimages.com*

curve, eating up the short straights between turns at high throttle, slinging the hard-sprung vehicle up Rimcrest with the skill of a professional racing driver. Which, in part, he was."

Five hundred fifty horsepower may be an exaggeration, as there are other sources that mention McQueen's "400-horse, Chevy-powered Jeep." Still, even 400 horsepower in a compact, military-derived, short-wheelbase 4×4. . . . Traco was an engine building concern in Southern California that prepared racing engines for Can-Am, Trans-Am,

Formula 5000, and other series. In its heyday, nobody could get more, and more reliable, horsepower out of a small-block Chevy V-8 than Traco. The engine in McQueen's Jeep was likely the venerable 350-ci version, perhaps bored and/or stroked to 370–380 ci. Generating 375–400 horsepower is believable for that type of engine and more than enough to make the sub-3,000-pound CJ spin like a top if McQueen wanted it to.

It is not known when he acquired it or who did the modifications, but some of the usual suspects were involved. The above-noted tooled leather interior was likely the work of Tony Nancy, who retrimmed several of McQueen's cars. And Chad McQueen clearly remembers that Von Dutch did the pinstriping, which traces the body lines. Sonny Bono later owned it during his tenure as mayor of Palm Springs, California.

Besides the legendary guys that worked on it, and of course its famous owner, this unique Jeep even has racing provenance, pressed into service at the last minute by McQueen, the off-road racer (see Chapter 3). Unfortunately, it is not known when he disposed of it, to whom, or where it resides today.

1969 Porsche 911S

It's one thing to find a much sought-after, highly original, low-mileage car that has remained in the same family for nearly four decades. It's yet another thing when that family's name is McQueen.

Porsche really stepped up the performance of its seminal 911 with the S model, introduced in 1967. The pre–safety bumper 911s of 1967–1973, particularly the S, combine everything that was good about a Porsche: classic styling, high build quality, rousing performance, motorsport success, and purity of purpose. Things got rough beginning in 1974: heavy

A classic portrait of a classic 911. Porschephiles seek out 1967–1973 911S models as their own Holy Grail. Finding an almost completely original example with less than 48,000 miles is one thing. Finding one special ordered and bought new by Steve McQueen would be another. *Matt Stone*

One detail that is nearly always missing is the rear muffler valance. Not that it looks that great, but it was a period factory option and most have been removed or were torn off along the way. This piece is present and accounted for on the McQueen S. Factory Slate Gray paint glows in the afternoon sun. *Evan Klein*

safety bumpers, emissions control equipment, decreased performance, funky fabric patterns and colors. It is for these reasons that the early cars are so prized by Porschephiles.

Nineteen sixty-nine was a big year for the 911. The wheelbase increased 2.25 inches in the name of improved ride, more stable handling, and more room inside. The S variant, again the top-of-the-line performer, got a power increase from 180 to 190 horsepower at 6,800 rpm—heady stuff at the time for a street-legal, 2.0-liter six-cylinder engine. So important was balance to the overall equation that Stuttgart's engineers specified two batteries, one mounted beneath each headlight, to distribute weight more evenly. The all-important 0-to-60-mile-per-hour run took just 6.5 seconds, as good as most American muscle cars of the day, although with handling the big-block behemoths couldn't

dream of matching. The price? Base MSRP was just $7,695. With options, most went out the door for around $8,500.

McQueen had run through three Ferraris by the time the new-and-improved 911s came out for 1969. The '69 S's combination of sportiness, power, and style must have done the trick for him, as he special ordered a Slate Gray example new in November 1968. It was a lightly optioned car—no fog lamps or air conditioning—although it is interesting to see a few luxury touches in place, such as the aluminum rear lower muffler valance and power sunroof. Although a Sportomatic semi-automatic transaxle was optional, there's no way McQueen would have anything other than the standard five-speed stick. The 911S wasn't the only Porsche in the McQueen household at the time, however, as Neile was driving a rare 1968 911L—one of only about 450 produced—although unlike her husband's Porsche, hers did have the Sportomatic trans.

This is not the 911 seen in the opening scenes of the film *Le Mans*, although there's no doubt this car inspired it. McQueen's Solar Productions purchased a similar car in Europe, an identically colored 1970 example (see Chapter 2). The reason? It's hard to say, other than it may have been easier to obtain another car for filming from the factory than to ship his personal driver from Southern California to France and back.

The Porsche stayed with McQueen throughout his moves from Brentwood to Malibu to Santa Paula, including two divorces and two subsequent marriages. The registration was in his name when he died. He willed the car to his daughter, Terry, and when she passed away in 1998, it went to Chad, rejoining the '58 Speedster in his garage.

What is most striking about this 911 is its level of originality. Its factory-applied Slate Gray paint is rich and shiny, yet wears a well-rubbed patina. The body gaps and door fits are factory tight. The chrome, glass, and rubber have a never-been-replaced, factory look, and the dull polish on those classic Fuchs alloy wheels looks just right. It even smells good—old German car smells.

Chad admits that his late sister let the car go a bit, but all it took was fastidious detailing and some mechanical servicing to bring it back to shape. The front seats were shot, so they've been reupholstered in factory-style black-patterned leather. His dad canted the tachometer to the left, race car style, so the top end of the rev range and the redline are more visible through the steering wheel. A later audio system and speakers, and a short-throw 911R shifter, have also been added, but other than that, McQueen's 911S is absolutely stock. The engine compartment is far from concours but is beautiful in that it retains all of Porsche's original finishes and stickers. The speedometer reads less than 48,000 miles.

Your author's own 911 is 20 years newer than this one, but the view is comfortably familiar as I settle into the driver's seat. This car is simpler than mine: no power windows, seats, or locks, no console, no A/C. The racing-style shift pattern of the earlier type 915 five-speed transmission puts first gear to

The author at the wheel of Steve (then Terry, now Chad) McQueen's 911S—a drive that won't be forgotten anytime soon. Note optional bright metal trim along the rocker panels and wheel arches. This car is often confused with a similar Porsche used in the filming of *Le Mans*, but that 911S was a '70 model purchased by McQueen in Europe (see Chapter 3). *Evan Klein*

"My dad drove the crap out of that thing," Chad recalls, yet this S-spec engine has never been apart and doesn't smoke a wisp. The engine compartment is as factory issued and would be a good pattern for how to restore one. It's strong too, good for nearly 1.5 horsepower per cubic inch. *Evan Klein*

the left and down, with gears two through five in the normal H pattern. No throttle is required to start the Bosch-injected flat six, just a twist of the key. And there it is: the horse bark of a small-displacement 911, before the effects of more cubic inches, heavier flywheels, or catalytic converters changed it.

As I'm riding in one of the most unique 911s on earth, I'm cautious pulling out on Pacific Coast Highway, not far from where McQueen lived in the Trancus area of Malibu. It only takes a few corners and a couple runs through the gears to be reminded of the magic of early 911s: telepathic steering, strong

McQueen's 911S was an early '69 model, indicated by VIN 119300193's first registration date in late November 1968, to his company, Solar Productions.

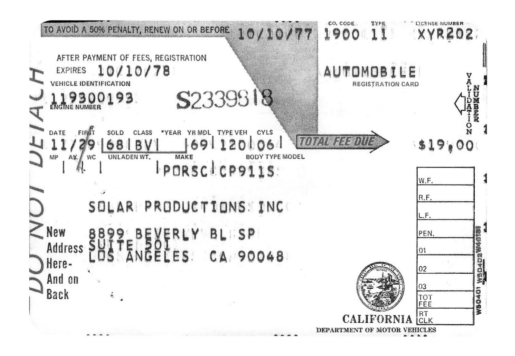

brake feel, minimal body roll, and a responsive powerplant that makes great, race-bred noises. This engine idles like a Rolex, yet revs freely to 7,000 rpm. These mechanical fuel-injection systems are known to pop and spit now and again, but McQueen's machine does no such thing. It feels impressively powerful for just two naturally aspirated liters; part of that is due to the early 911's relatively light weight of around 2,400 pounds. There isn't much torque to be had below 2,500 rpm, but it's sweet from there on, and the engine brightens considerably at 5,000 revs.

I didn't push the car hard enough to risk the early 911's infamous off-throttle oversteer, as I had no desire to pitch its tail off a narrow Malibu canyon road. The shifter is better than on many of these cars I've driven, perhaps due to minimal linkage wear because of such low mileage. This car is tight and generally rattle free too; there's nothing like a car that's never been crashed or taken apart. There's no replacement for originality and the gentle, honest patina that a car acquires only over years of well-cared-for use.

When I brought Steve McQueen's 911S back to its garage, I let it idle for while, just to soak in the vibes for a moment longer. There was nobody sitting in the passenger seat, yet somehow, I knew I hadn't been alone as I sliced through the same canyons that McQueen used to in this very car.

1952 Hudson Wasp

It was clear that many cars appealed to McQueen not just for their performance potential but for their design and aesthetics. One such machine was this Hudson Wasp coupe. It is an unusual example of the step-down Hudson for several reasons. The first is that it is a Wasp model, not the more well-known Hornet. However, it has the rare Twin-H Power dual-carb setup not often seen on a Wasp. Twin-H was Hudson's way of competing with the V-8 engines that were being introduced by most other manufacturers at the time. Hudson just didn't have the money to develop its own V-8 after World War II, but the dual-carb, flathead six was plenty quick for its day, enjoying considerable success in the early days of NASCAR. Another element that made McQueen's Wasp unique was the automatic transmission, as a majority of Twin-H-equipped Hudsons had manual transmissions.

McQueen owned the car later in his life; these Barbara Minty McQueen photos were taken at the *continued on page 60*

McQUEEN'S SHELBY COBRA —OR WAS IT?

The original Shelby Cobra needs little introduction here or anywhere else. And it's no surprise that Steve McQueen, being able to afford virtually any automobile he wanted in 1963, turned up at Shelby American looking at one of Carroll Shelby's Ford-powered sports cars. The 289-ci, 271-horsepower first-generation Cobra was capable of running with—and often beating—cars like the Corvette, Jaguar E-Type, and most road-going Ferraris. McQueen is known to have had a Cobra for several years during this time period, but was it really his?

According to the Shelby American Automobile Club Registry, a dictionary-sized tome published about every 10 years, documenting the ownership history of a variety of Shelby Cobras and Mustangs, plus Ford GTs, the answer is no. This photo, taken at Shelby's Los Angeles area race shop in June 1963, shows Carroll Shelby and McQueen inspecting this car, chassis number CSX2174. Shelby American photographer Dave Friedman recalls that McQueen visited the shop for a few days prior to taking delivery of this car. But he didn't buy it.

According to the 1997 edition of the SAAC Registry, "Shelby, a friend of McQueen's, felt that several months of use would convince McQueen to purchase the car. When he showed no interest in doing so, the car was returned to the factory at Shelby's request and was invoiced on 4/14/64 to the Francis Motor Car Company (Portland, Oregon)." The car led a somewhat sordid history from there, but that's not germane to McQueen's time with it. Photos exist of McQueen with the car on movie sets in 1963, although the wheels had been painted black, and the dual, rear-exit exhaust system had been swapped for pipes that exited just in front of the rear wheels. Another clue supporting the fact that McQueen never owned the Cobra shows in this photo from a 1999 spread in *Barracuda* magazine: the license is a manufacturer plate, indicating that Shelby American still owned the car.

Dave Friedman

Real-Man Revisited

CALIFORNIA
1D MEG 013

Barracuda *magazine*

Just another day at the airport, as McQueen hoses down the approach to his hangar while he has his morning coffee, his comfy old Hudson Wasp two-door sedan in the background. *Barbara Minty McQueen*

continued from page 57
Santa Paula airport in 1979, and it was sold in the 1984 estate auction in Las Vegas. The Wasp went through a number of owners, most recently auctioned at the McQueen sale that took place at the Petersen Automotive Museum in November 2006. It was purchased by that institution to add to its collection of star cars.

Barbara affectionately recalls the Hudson as McQueen's "Sunday-go-to-church car." He was done with his racing days by then, perhaps preferring the Hudson's warm, comfortable nature. At the time of its purchase by the Petersen, it was in largely original condition and had developed a wonderful, honest, if slightly worn look. Sure, there is some rust, the chrome is slightly pitted, and the paint has been polished through to the metal in a few places. But its bodywork is arrow straight, the odometer reading just over 63,000 original miles.

"My dad drove that Hudson everywhere, for years," Chad later recalled. "I remember him picking me up from school in it. He loved that thing."

1949 Cadillac Series 62

Dale Walksler is, primarily, a motorcycle aficionado. He attended the McQueen estate auction in 1984 looking to purchase a few of the late actor's bikes, and he did (see Chapter 4). What he hadn't planned on was buying a car. Yet this big Caddy sedan won him over.

"The motorcycle prices went quickly beyond my estimation. In retrospect, they were great deals," says Walksler of the auction. "This was the first year for Cadillac's new overhead-valve V-8. And the 1949 Cadillac was also *Motor Trend* magazine's first Car of the Year. When lot 518 came up, I couldn't resist McQueen's hubcap-less Cadillac for only $5,500."

Walksler and the friend who attended the auction with him hadn't made any advance plans for transporting an automobile from the Las Vegas auction to his home in North Carolina. "So, we decided to drive it home and did so, with no problems whatsoever." He even located the hubcaps. No doubt McQueen would be pleased that the adventurous pair decided to put his car on the road, not on the back of a truck, for the trek home.

Today, Walksler runs the Wheels Through Time Museum in Maggie Valley, North Carolina. He still owns the Cadillac, and several of his motorcycles.

The Wasp as it looked in November 2006, just prior to its purchase by the Petersen Automotive Museum. The Hudson shows its years, yet wears most of its original paint and chrome. *Matt Stone*

McQueen's 1949 Cadillac sedan was sold at his 1984 estate auction. It was purchased by Dale Walksler and remains in his Wheels Through Time Museum. Nineteen forty-nine was a breakthrough year for Cadillac, when the Wreath and Crest brand introduced its first overhead-valve V-8 engine, the most powerful in American production at the time, which no doubt impressed McQueen. *Wheels Through Time Museum*

Significant Others

Besides the more iconic cars that Steve McQueen is noted for owning, there were so many more that came and went.

Nearly everyone had a VW Beetle at one time or another, and several McQueen biographies make reference to him owning one too. There was also a faded-green mid-1950s Chevy Nomad wagon, reportedly nicknamed *The Funk* by McQueen. He often negotiated the use of a car or motorcycle during the filming of a movie and ended up owning it when production came to a close. Such was the case during the making of *The War Lover* in 1961.

"My agent had a special bit written into my contract," said McQueen. "He had the studio agree to provide me with a limousine and chauffeur to get me to the set. But that wasn't my thing, and I told the studio people, 'Why not let me buy a small car

and drive it myself?' This saved them money so they okayed the offer. As a result, I got me a twelve-speed, four-wheel-drive Land Rover, which I shipped back to California after the film was over. I came out ahead on the deal." Chad recalls that the Land Rover was green. It spent most of its time at the McQueens' home near Palm Springs, and there were plenty of places to take it off-roading nearby.

We're not sure if McQueen's time in the military, or all the war-era characters he played, had any effect on his acquisition, in the late 1960s, of a U.S. Army surplus half-track truck. But it was one vehicle Chad recalls with a chuckle. "This thing was huge, with regular wheels and tires on the front, and tank treads on the back," he says. "It was olive drab camouflage, and as with so many of his other cars, Dad had Von Dutch pinstripe it. Dad took all of the bench seats out and put in four rows of Solar racing buckets [see Chapter 2]. He always kept it at our

The McQueens bought this '57 Bel Air convertible, equipped with the rare and desirable fuel-injected 283-ci V-8 either new or shortly thereafter. "I think it was mostly my mom's car," recalls Chad, no surprise considering that it's equipped with an automatic, as opposed to the Steve McQueen–preferred manual transmission. It's currently owned by Kent and Ruth Buzzi Perkins, the latter of *Rowan & Martin's Laugh-In* fame. *Matt Stone*

place in Palm Springs, and I remember going out to the drive-in movies in it." No average sport/utility vehicle for the McQueen family.

Although he applied himself with vigor to anything he attempted, McQueen wasn't about attracting attention. This is why he often used a phony name when he entered motorcycle races, most of his cars were painted dark colors, and the Mercedes-Benz 300 SEL 6.3 was his kind of sedan.

Mercedes' full-sized four-door was an upright and proud machine, the choice of conservative bank presidents the world over. The design had been around since the early 1960s, powered by a variety of six-cylinder engines. In late 1967, Daimler-Benz gave the old girl the same treatment that many American carmakers did in creating the original muscle cars: take a big engine out of a big car and install it in a smaller one. The Mercedes 600 Pullman and Limo used a powerful 6.3-liter fuel-injected,

single overhead cam V-8, and with a little work, it found its way under the hood of the 300 SEL.

Packing 300 SAE gross horsepower attached to a four-speed automatic transmission, it was capable of 0-to-60-mile-per-hour runs of less than seven seconds and 150-mile-per-hour cruising speeds. This top-of-the-line model received every option Mercedes offered at the time, including air suspension, leather upholstery, air conditioning, four-wheel disc brakes, and hand-cut wood interior trim.

Chad picks up the story: "Sometime in 1972, I remember a transporter pulling up to our house in Brentwood. They unloaded a big black Mercedes-Benz four-door. I said, 'Dad, what are you going to do with that?' He said, 'This fucking thing is so fast, you wouldn't believe it.'" They walked around the back, and Chad saw that it was a 300 SEL 6.3. McQueen the younger commented that he'd never heard of one and asked his father where he'd seen it. Steve replied,

"Last month when I was in Germany, I was in a 911S doing about a hundred thirty on the autobahn, and I saw something coming up behind flashing its lights. It must have been doing a hundred fifty miles per hour." "He moved over and looked over his shoulder, and here was this 60-year-old guy in a cap smoking a pipe, and he went blowing by him like he was standing still. So he decided right there that he needed to 'buy me one of those.'" Chad recalls that "it was one of his favorite cars. He drove that thing everywhere."

Steve McQueen's first Porsche was the above-noted Speedster. The car he drove in the movie *Le Mans* was a top-of-the-line 911S, and he had a nearly identical car at home. So, when Porsche came out with a production turbocharged 911, it was no surprise that McQueen had to have one. The 911 Turbo bowed in the U.S. market for the 1976

model year, and McQueen bought one finished in the same Slate Gray as his 1969 911S.

Sitting squat on its wide Pirelli P7 low-profile tires stuffed beneath widely flared fenders, the new Turbo was one of the baddest rides of the mid-1970s. Its flamboyant rear whale-tail spoiler is still a Porsche trademark touch three decades later. The Turbo's not-so-naturally aspirated 3.0-liter flat six was rated at 234 horsepower. This doesn't sound like much these days, but considering that year's Corvette was only good for a measly 180, the Porsche was a legitimate rocket, running 0-to-60 miles per hour in just five seconds.

Chad was learning to drive by that time and snuck out with the Porsche a few times to, er, practice his technique for driving a manual transmission. He recalls one instance when his dad called him

This mongrel 911 is a mystery. The rear badge (not shown) identifies it as a 911E, the midrange offering, and other cues point to it being a '71 model. But several parts have been jumbled around from earlier and later 911s. It also wears wheels and hubcaps most often seen on four-cylinder 912s. This photo was taken near his Malibu home in 1979, prior to McQueen and wife-to-be Barbara Minty moving to Santa Paula. *Barbara Minty McQueen*

Craig Barrett is now the proud owner of McQueen's 930. "Dad only had that car for about a year; I'm not really sure why he sold it," recalls Chad. The owner who purchased it out of Dino Martin's estate repainted it in the factory Slate Gray but didn't complete the restoration. Barrett purchased it from him in 1995, completed the job, and freshened the engine. The odo read just under 150,000 miles when these photos were taken, but the car looks, feels, and performs like new. *Matt Stone*

from out of town, ending their chat with, "I'll see you day after tomorrow." The following day, Chad snuck the Turbo out for a few runs down the narrow street near their Malibu home. "There it was, a Yellow cab, with my dad inside, coming the other way up the street. I could see those blue eyes just blazing out at me from the back seat. I think he came home a day early knowing he might catch me screwing up or something. He was upset, but he was cool about it. He sent me to my room to think about what I'd done. That car really hauled." McQueen kept the car a few years, then sold it to Dino Martin (son of Dean) and his girlfriend, champion figure skater Dorothy Hamill.

Ferraris, Porsches, and a Jaguar XK-SS—dark colors or otherwise—weren't the best tools to help one of the world's most recognized movie stars cut a low profile. By the early 1970s, McQueen was looking for ways to fly further below the radar. One was his 1958 GMC pickup. Long before it was restored and repainted in a brilliant blue, it was just another rundown workhorse.

For a time after his divorce from Neile, McQueen maintained a suite at the Beverly Wilshire Hotel and kept several of his cars parked in its garage (not to mention a motorcycle or two inside his room). The ratty GMC was among them. Barbara kept the GMC after McQueen's passing, selling it at auction in November 2006. Although it looked spectacular, it's a shame it doesn't still wear the original, forlorn patina it did when McQueen used it as stealth transport.

McQueen bought a new Rolls-Royce in 1978. This was an unusual move, as McQueen seldom

This GMC styleside was one McQueen's Beverly Hills cruisers in the 1970s. It was in much more battle-scarred condition back then but was later restored. The Jimmy must have been a hit among the valets at the Beverly Wilshire Hotel, where McQueen kept six to eight cars at any given time. Naturally, it too had the largest V-8 engine that GMC offered in 1958. *Matt Stone*

McQueen's properties in Santa Paula, California, and Ketchum, Idaho, were littered with hard-working pickups of all manner. There were Chevys, GMCs, and these two wonderfully shop-worn Fords; the yellow one is a 1957, the blue and white one with the camper shell, oversized rolling stock, and Perlux driving lights a 1968. With a beard and cowboy hat, McQueen could have gotten away as being just another rancher. Almost.
Barbara Minty McQueen

went for cars that shouted wealth or status. But it was a spontaneous purchase . . . and one that he nearly forgot. Barbara recalls that the couple walked past a Rolls dealer in L.A. one day, and he said, "Come on, let's go inside." He ordered a black Corniche convertible on the spot. Months later, the dealership called and said, "Mr. McQueen, your Rolls-Royce is ready." He replied, "I never ordered a Rolls." The dealer read him back all of his credit information. He replied, "Well, I guess I did. Where do I pick it up?" Chad adds that "back from where my dad came from, always being poor, a Rolls represented that you had made it. That's probably why he agreed to buy the car."

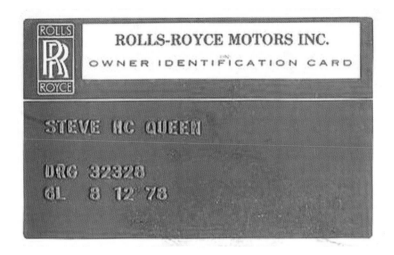

McQueen was a reluctant Roller but made the plunge and bought his first and only example of "The Best Car In The World" in 1978. *Barbara Minty McQueen*

Barbara tells another humorous story about it in her book, in a subchapter called *King of Uncool*: "Whenever we jumped into his convertible Rolls-Royce for a ride, Steve had only one cassette tape in his player and that was from one of his favorite movies, *Saturday Night Fever*. The first song that blared out of the speakers was the disco anthem 'Stayin' Alive,' which John Travolta immortalized in the film's opening scene. Usually, I ducked under the dashboard and tried to be as inconspicuous as possible when it played, but one time, it was too much, and I let Steve have it." McQueen had also permed his hair about that time, all of which proves that even an icon of masculine style can hit a rough patch.

When McQueen and Barbara moved to Santa Paula, a sparsely populated farm community a few hours north of Los Angeles, in 1979, they purchased a ranch house on about 15 acres of land. By that time, McQueen had become enamored with vintage aircraft and was taking flying lessons. In order to house his first plane, the McQueens maintained a hangar at the Santa Paula airport. The hangar became a focal point of their lives, as the couple lived there while their new house was being remodeled. "In the morning, we'd open up that big door, lay in bed, have a cup of coffee, and watch life and the airplanes go by."

Many of McQueen's cars and motorcycles were stored there, plus an ever-growing collection of antiques, signs, posters, furniture, photographs, gas pumps, motorcycle parts, and vintage toy cars and bikes. During the last years of his life, McQueen went on a collecting binge, buying vintage automobiles and motorcycles at a furious rate. The Santa Paula home and the airport hangar became his toy box, and he worked vigorously at filling it up. Over time, he acquired a 1951 Hudson Hornet sedan to go along with the Wasp coupe, a Chrysler Hemi-powered 1953 Allard, a 1949 Cadillac four-door, a 1931 Lincoln Club Sedan, a 1935 Chrysler Airflow, a 1930 Cadillac V-8 Coupe, a WWII-era military Willys jeep, and three Packards: a 1939 Super 8 four-door sedan, a 1940 Packard 120 Convertible coupe, and a rare Packard Super 8 Convertible coupe. The properties were also scattered with a variety of pickups, mostly early 1950s Chevrolets. These in addition to the XK-SS, several Porsches, and the cars he'd kept after the filming of several movies.

Between that little MG TC of 1952 and the formidable collection of machinery he had amassed by the time he passed away in late 1980, Steve McQueen had owned around 40 cars, not including many used as movie props and driven by his wives. Some were ordinary. Many were extraordinary. Today, they would comprise a multi-million-dollar collection that any ardent enthusiast would be proud to own. But Steve McQueen loved his two- and four-wheel pursuits not for their value or what they said about him to the outside world. He loved them because of the magic of the machine and the freedom that came with driving and riding, often as fast as he or they could go.

What did cars mean to Steve McQueen? Although he was sitting aboard a motorcycle when he said it, this quote likely applies to his four-wheeled pursuits as well: "Billy Graham once asked me what my religion was, and I told him, 'It's the desert, the grass, the sun in the sky—and my wheels.'" Is there a truer definition of "car guy"?

It's amazing that McQueen waited until his late 40s to get into flying, considering his prowess at other manly pursuits such as motorcycle racing, martial arts, and guns. But instead of the latest winged machines, McQueen went in for vintage aircraft, earning his private pilot's license in July 1979. He would often hold court at his Santa Paula airport hangar, and pictured here are three of his planes. Unlike most pilots, who start out small, McQueen's first airplane was a 1941 Boeing Stearman in traditional yellow. The Stearman was also known as the PT-17 Kaydet in its role as a military trainer during World War II. McQueen purchased his example, powered by the Continental W670 nine-cylinder radial engine, almost on a whim in 1979: Steve did not yet have his pilot's license. Among the last of McQueen's six airplanes was this silver and blue 1945 Boeing Stearman; the custom registration number (3188) was said to be his reform-school identification. The two-passenger Stearman was typically piloted from the rear open cockpit.

Sammy Mason, a famous and immensely experienced flight instructor, was brought out of near retirement to teach McQueen how to fly. McQueen's love of fine, rare machinery is no more evident than in his purchase of one of the last Pitcairn Mailwings known to survive. A near derelict in the mid-1970s, McQueen's PA-8 Mailwing was one of six built in the early 1930s to serve the fledgling air-mail system. The Pitcairn company, now better known for its line of autogyros, held a reputation for building strong and meticulously finished aircraft. Cognizant of its importance in history, McQueen did not fly the Pitcairn as often as he did his more common Stearman biplane. *Barbara Minty McQueen*

Chapter 2

McQUEEN ON SCREEN

Steve McQueen's talent at the wheel of an automobile or

aboard a motorcycle was considerable. He was ultra competitive at anything he did, and mastering cars and bikes became an early passion. By the time he was able to influence the content of the films he appeared in and create opportunities for his characters to drive or ride interesting machinery, he had already done a considerable amount of racing at amateur and semi-professional levels (see Chapter 3).

Even in early films, where McQueen wasn't in a position to weigh in on the script, he was often seen at the wheel—a place that came naturally to him. He drove a Ford in *The Blob* (1958) and was Frank Sinatra's chauffeur in the war movie *Never So Few* (1959), piloting a military jeep, of course. But the first opportunity for movie-goers to get a real look at McQueen's love for all things motorized happened to be in the film that most consider his breakthrough role.

The Great Escape (1963)

As you'll read about in the next chapter, Steve McQueen's amateur racing career was in full bloom by the spring of 1962. He'd enjoyed success in the production classes running his Porsche Speedster and later moved up to a Lotus XI sports racer, then a Cooper Formula Junior open-wheeled machine. He was offered a factory ride and was seriously toying with the notion of turning pro. But his acting career was bursting at the seams as well. McQueen was on the glide path to stardom.

The Great Escape. MGM/CORBIS

Four members of *Escape*'s dream cast: from left, James Coburn, James Garner, McQueen—at the handlebars, of course—and director John Sturges. The three actors remained lifelong friends, and each was a genuine car guy. *United Artists/Photofest*

His performance in 1960's *The Magnificent Seven* was a standout, and he was lauded for his work in *The War Lover*. His days of small parts and secondary billing were over, and it was inevitable that his involvement in racing would get in the way sooner or later. It came to a boil when the studio sent an attorney to McQueen's doorstep with what was tantamount to a restraining order, written to keep him off the track or risk his contract. It was racing or the movies.

"They gave me twenty-four hours to make up my mind. I took most of those twenty-four hours thinking about whether I wanted to go on racing, earning my money on the track, or whether I wanted to continue being an actor on the studio's terms. It was a very tough decision for me to reach. Still, I had Neile and our two young children to consider, and that made the difference. I signed their paper." It's a good thing too; otherwise, he may never have made *The Great Escape*.

An iconic shot of McQueen as Captain Virgil Hilts, aboard the faux German military bike. "Halt?" Not Hilts. Or McQueen. *Bettmann/CORBIS*

Chad McQueen recalls: "My old man wasn't stupid. He probably looked at what he could make as a race driver, even under the best conditions, and what he could earn as an actor, and it was pretty clear." As demonstrated throughout the 1960s and especially in 1969 and 1970, McQueen would find other ways to feed his high-speed addiction, even if he had to form his own production company and build an entire film around motorsport.

The Magnificent Seven's ensemble male cast framework was a hit, so more than a little of its makeup carried over into *The Great Escape*. John Sturges directed both and would figure in later McQueen films. Charles Bronson, James Coburn, and McQueen all appeared in *Seven* and were signed for *Escape*. But *Seven*'s principal star, Yul Brynner, was nowhere to be seen. Instead, Steve McQueen was the headliner. The film is based on the true story of a group of Allied officers, primarily British, who escape a Nazi prison camp.

"John and I worked a hairy motorcycle chase into the script," said McQueen. His character, Captain Virgil Hilts, was not unlike himself. Hilts was a bit of a loner and on the mischievous side, yet a man of character with a good heart, who ultimately helps save the day. He spent a lot of time in solitary confinement, known as the "cooler," hence his nickname "The Cooler King." "The idea was this Cooler King character makes good his escape by stealing a cycle, gets chased cross-country by German cyclists and loses them by jumping this big barbed-wire fence with this bike."

Biographer Nolan summarizes what McQueen accomplished strategically with this film. "By inserting this cycle sequence into *The Great Escape*, Steve had out-foxed the studio; now the executives had no choice. Steve *would* race. On film, and at *their* risk." Production took place in Germany, near Munich, and in the countryside surrounding the Rhine. It was just a few years earlier that McQueen had discovered off-road cycle riding, so the scenario was a natural for him.

WWII-era BMW motorcycles never could have taken the punishment the stunt crew had planned for them, so special bikes were built for the job. "We had four bikes for this film. I was running a forty-cubic-inch Triumph TT special. We painted it olive drab and put on a luggage rack and an old seat to make it look like a wartime BMW. The first time we tried out the bikes at full chat, the Bavarians just gaped, open-mouthed. They didn't believe a bike could go that fast over this kind of uphill-downhill terrain."

McQueen's off-road motorcycle muse and stunt double, Bud Ekins—a name you'll read often in this book—was there. How did the two become connected? Ekins explains, "He bought a motorcycle from me in about 1960 or '61. I was a Triumph dealer. Actor Dick Powell's son, Norman, had bought a Triumph Bonneville from me, and his wife said he couldn't have it. So he sold it to McQueen. They came in together to check and see that if McQueen bought the bike, would the warranty still be valid. I said sure, no problem. Movie stars don't work all year around, and Steve started hanging around the shop. He saw all these bikes around there that didn't have lights on them and they had number plates and all that kinda crap. He wanted to know what that was all about, so I told him about desert racing. I asked him to come out with us; he came out one time, and that was it."

How did Ekins get from the deserts of Southern California to Bavaria? "He just asked one day. He said, 'I'm going to Germany and I'm going to make a movie. Do you want to come over and double me? There's some motorcycle work in it.' I said, 'sure,' and that was about it. That was all I heard for a month or two, then he called up and asked if I had a suit? I said, 'Yeah. Why?' He said, 'Well put it on. I'm going to pick you up and introduce you to the director.' He showed up—in Levis and a T-shirt, of course—and here I am in a suit. We drove to the studio in that Jag of his. We met John Sturges, and he kinda looked at me and nodded his head, and then I went to Germany about three weeks later. I was there for three months. That was the first movie I ever worked on."

The audience got a hint that there may be motorcycle madness later in the film when Hilts was speaking with another soldier while the two were neighbors in solitary confinement. Hilts said he'd done some racing. His cellblock mate asked, "Horse racing?" Hilts replied, "Motorcycles. Flat

Hilts, not long after he trips up a German soldier on the road, stealing his bike, uniform, and weapon. *United Artists/MPTV.net*

tracks. County fairs. Picked up a buck here and there. Helped pay my tuition."

The bike play takes place late in the movie. Hilts had already cleared the prison camp fences, heading for the freedom of Switzerland. He figured the quickest way there was on two wheels, so he strung some wire across the road, into which rode a hapless German soldier (the stunt was performed by Ekins), taking quite a tumble. Hilts stole the bike, the rider's uniform, and weapon. The escapee was soon discovered at a border security station, and the chase was on.

"Steve did a helluva lot of that riding himself," says Ekins. "I really didn't do much of it. Anything where he may get hurt, that's what I did. But all the other stuff, when you see him riding by, he did all

that himself and was enjoying it very much. There's a chase sequence in there where the Germans were after him, and he was so much a better rider than they were, that he just ran away from them. And you weren't going to slow him down. So, they put a German uniform on him, and he chased himself! I rode as a German soldier too, but he chased himself several times in the movie."

There was one scene in which McQueen didn't ride, and it is the one for which *The Great Escape* is best known. Hemmed in on all sides by several German soldiers on motorcycles, barbed-wire fencing, and obstacles, Hilts knew there's only one way out—one that the others wouldn't dare follow. By now, he'd shed the German uniform and wore just khakis and a T-shirt. He surveyed the barrier, grit

One of the most iconic stunts in movie history was captured in this perfectly timed photograph, as McQueen's pal and stunt double Bud Ekins sails the German military bike née Triumph over a tall wood and barbed-wire (really string and rubber bands) fence. Planning pays off, as the stunt was captured in one take, with no damage to man or machine. *United Artists/MPTV.net*

his teeth, and gunned the faux-BMW toward the fence. Bike and rider dropped down into a dip, climbed the grassy bank at great speed, and sailed over the fence to a perfect landing.

There was no computer animation in those days, and the only way to make the 60-foot jump look right was to do it. Recall that McQueen had only just begun riding off-road bikes and wasn't quite up to the task. He tried a few times and couldn't get it right. "I always felt a little guilty about that," he said a decade later. "A lot of people thought it was me making that jump, but I've never tried to hide the truth about it. I could handle the jump now, I'm sure. Back in '62, I just didn't quite have the savvy." In spite of the fact that the image of McQueen flying through the air over a barbed-wire fence is among those he is most often identified with, it was Ekins aboard that flying Triumph.

The shot took a lot of measuring, estimating, and practice beforehand. The stunt crew kept massaging the contours of the hill that would be Ekins' launching pad, and the barbed wire was replaced with string, to minimize risk to the rider should something go wrong. Fortunately, nothing did. Ekins nailed the iconic stunt on the first take. Movie history made.

What of that now legendary motorcycle? "I sold it to a stuntman," recalls Ekins. Last time they had contact, the buyer said he didn't own the bike anymore. "He didn't know what he had. I didn't tell him it was the bike from *The Great Escape*." Movie history lost. Not only was *The Great Escape* the first film that showed the world—in a big way—that Steve McQueen loved bikes and was a spectacular rider, *Escape* was also a box office smash and vaulted him from the level of rising star to major star.

The motorhead actor had arrived.

The Thomas Crown Affair
(1968)

Thomas Crown was the role Steve McQueen was not supposed to be able to play. Crown was a wealthy Boston business tycoon who masterminded bank heists for the sport of it. He was rich, cultured, wore tailored suits, lived in a mansion, and flew a glider for fun. Growing up, McQueen was none of the above. He was at the height of his popularity and ability as an actor but had gotten there playing "regular Joe" type characters, most often cowboys or soldiers. Yet for all of his wealth and power, Thomas Crown was a bit of a loner. And this was something McQueen could identify with in making the character his own.

Neile explained in Turner Classic Movies' *Essence of Cool* documentary how McQueen landed the role: "Stan Kamen, his agent, said to me, 'We've got to get him out of those cowboy clothes. I want to see him as a sophisticated man.' There was a script out called *The Crown Caper*. Norman Jewison was directing it. Stan said, 'You've got to get him to do it.'

"One day we were having breakfast, and I said, 'It's too bad that Norman doesn't want you for this movie he's making.' Steve said, 'Who told you that?!' I said, 'Well, everybody's gotten a script. Rock Hudson, Sean Connery, all the guys who are sort of sophisticated.' So he started calling Norman."

Jewison recalled their conversation—"I said, 'Steve, this guy's elegant, he plays polo, and this is

A classed-up McQueen, the sexily elegant Dunaway, and Rolls-Royce's new Silver Shadow coupe set the tone for *The Thomas Crown Affair*. Note the Massachusetts license plate reading "TC 100" for Thomas Crown, of course; this was before most states offered personalized license plates. *MPTV.net*

The Thomas Crown Affair Rolls-Royce today. The paint has been redone in the original nonmetallic navy blue, but the engine and interior are slightly worn, yet original spec. It has since been purchased by the Petersen Automotive Museum to add to its growing collection of McQueen's machines. *Matt Stone*

going to be very hard for you,' and he said that was exactly why he wanted to do it." McQueen pulled it off with aplomb, cementing his stardom and underscoring his ability to apply himself and deliver a stretch-roll performance. His fiery costar was Faye Dunaway, who had just completed her breakout role in *Bonnie and Clyde.* She played insurance investigator Vicki Anderson, Crown's nemesis and love interest.

The Thomas Crown Affair not only proved that McQueen could act beyond his personal experiences, it also was the film that first showed movie audiences McQueen's deep and genuine affinity for automobiles.

There were three star cars in this slickly produced film. The first was Thomas Crown's daily driver, a 1967 Rolls-Royce Silver Shadow Coupé— an elegant, two-door version of the current Silver Shadow sedan. Chassis number CRX2672, a factory left-hand-drive example, was painted an appropriate shade of navy blue, with a buff-colored leather interior. Every Shadow Coupé was built to order, and the bodies were crafted at HJ Mulliner Park Ward Limited, an amalgam of two popular prewar coachbuilders. This ever-elegant Rolls was available in a convertible version (subsequently named the Corniche, one of which McQueen later owned) and could also be had as a Bentley coupe or convertible.

Power came courtesy of Rolls' standard-issue 6.2-liter all-aluminum overhead-valve (OHV) V-8; this was back in the day when the company could get away with declaring that its horsepower output was "adequate" and its torque rating "sufficient," but most guess it was good for around 250 horses and at least 300 lb-ft of torque. The smooth, quiet V-8 was backed by an automatic transmission, and power windows, brakes, steering, and a host of other luxury touches were standard, naturally. It wouldn't be a Rolls-Royce without a cabin well dressed in burr walnut veneer, Connolly leather, and footwells full of Wilton carpets—an appropriate ride for an upper-crust bank robber.

CRX2672 appears throughout *The Thomas Crown Affair*, most often with McQueen at the wheel. One notable scene shows Crown taking Vicki to his mansion on a rainy evening. The Rolls looks entirely at home in this environment—a cozy way for two beautiful people to travel as they're about to consummate their relationship. It sticks out more during the day, especially when Crown drives it to a cemetery to collect bags of money from his latest bank job. It plays another important role near the end of the film, when Anderson, the FBI, and the police plan to snare Crown for his crimes. The Rolls again ambles into and through the cemetery, but as the law closes in, it seems the car is only being driven by one of Crown's employees; Crown himself has already made his escape.

According to Bonhams, the auction company that most recently sold it, the Rolls was ordered new in 1967 by Hollywood film producer and writer Jerry Bresler. It is not clear how the Rolls came to be used in *Crown*, as Bresler is not credited as being involved with the production of the film. Perhaps he knew the producers and either lent or rented it to them, as it was appropriate for the need. Bresler passed away in 1977; it is believed the car was sold by his estate around 1980 to a woman who owned it into the

McQueen in Thomas Crown's Corvair-powered dune buggy was like a kid with a new toy: he played with it hard, enjoyed it a bunch, and broke it at least a time or three. Note the original Corvair air cleaner poking out from behind the Manx's rear deck. This movie license plate reads "TC 300." Since the Rolls-Royce was "TC 100," was Mr. Crown supposed to have yet another car? Not that we're aware of. *MPTV.net*

1990s. From there, it changed hands again, before being sold at the previously noted Bonhams sale in November 2006 to the Petersen Automotive Museum in Los Angeles.

Thomas Crown's other car could not be more of a contrast to a deep-blue Rolls-Royce and underscores McQueen's influence in the vehicles used for his films. In a period documentary about the making of the film, McQueen told the story of the red dune buggy that so clearly demonstrated his love of cars and his driving talent: "Crown lives at the beach, and he has a sand dune buggy. I helped 'em design it, so I'm kinda proud of that. It's set on a Volkswagen chassis, with big ol' wide weenies—big wide tires on mag wheels, Corvair engine stuffed in the back, semi-reclining position somewhat like on a Formula 1 car. It's very light, you know. It's pulling about 230 horses, and the vehicle weighs about 1,000 pounds."

Designer/musician/surfer Bruce Meyers wanted something fun, light, and inexpensive to take to the beach. No such vehicle existed in the early 1960s, so he created one. Employing a playfully attractive fiberglass body, a purpose-built chassis, and a Volkswagen engine, his Meyers Manx single-handedly launched the dune buggy phenomenon. The chassis and suspension proved too expensive for the low-cost kits that Meyers wanted to sell, so he adapted the design to fit a shortened VW floorpan.

Although dozens of other companies ripped off Meyers' idea and built their own variations, Crown's dune buggy was built using an original Meyers Manx body. According to an article by Timothy Paul Barton that appeared in the April 2005 issue of *Kit Car Builder* magazine, the Crown buggy was built up by a company called Con-Ferr. Barton said the script called for a Jeep. But McQueen had seen a Meyers Manx flying through the air on the cover of a 1966 issue of *Hot Rod* magazine and apparently felt it was more Thomas Crown's style.

The bright-red body was modified in numerous ways, the most obvious being the wraparound windscreen, sunken headlights beneath plastic covers, and the luggage rack on the back. Like most Manxes, the Crown buggy employed a Volkswagen floorpan, swingarm rear suspension, and four-speed

VW transaxle. The "big ol' wide weenies" McQueen mentions are Firestone racing tires (Indy 500 super speedway rubber, purchased from race team owner Andy Granatelli) on specially cast American Racing wheels. As with many of his personal cars, McQueen tapped Tony Nancy to stitch the custom leather seats and interior trim. The seat frames came from a Datsun Fairlady sports car, and it's likely that this Manx had one of the nicest interiors ever installed in a dune buggy.

What really set Crown's Manx apart was its powerplant. Most such buggies ran an air-cooled VW flat four. Depending on the state of tune, power outputs for these engines ranged from 40 to perhaps 125 horses; most dune buggies were built using relatively stock engines with about 75 to 100 horsepower—not good enough for McQueen. So this one was built using a Chevrolet Corvair's horizontally opposed, air-cooled six-cylinder engine. As noted above, McQueen claims the engine was "pulling about 230 horses," although author Barton said it was more like 140, the four-carb Corvair engine's stock output. Even taking the conservative estimate, the Crown buggy had a power-to-weight ratio rivaling some race cars. It was fast.

The muscled-up Manx appears in *The Thomas Crown Affair* several times, all at the beach, of course. Its most famous scene is several minutes long and shows Crown and Anderson assaulting the dunes. Most impressive is that there were no stunt doubles used for any of it: McQueen did all the driving, with Faye Dunaway in the passenger seat. The scene is a gem and again demonstrated that Steve McQueen was both fabulous driver and certified car freak. To watch him spin the buggy around on the sand, splash water, chase birds, launch over a dune, and fly the buggy through the air is like watching a beaming child play with a new toy. A camera was mounted in the back of the Manx for cutaway shots, which clearly show both actors in the buggy as it careened around the beach. McQueen could turn the camera on and off via a hidden switch.

Some of the action was ad-libbed, McQueen just driving the buggy as he wished. Other elements were more carefully thought through. "What I've got to do," McQueen said, "is to take the sand dune

McQueen said costar Faye Dunaway was "a trooper." Since so many of the scenes were shot close up or from the buggy itself, there was no way to double either actor effectively, so McQueen drove and Dunaway was along for the ride, which got wild more than a few times. *United Artists/Photofest*

buggy and drop it straight down [the dune], and then run the rim around the outside of it." The move worked to great effect, spraying sand everywhere.

Faye Dunaway proved a more than good sport about the whole deal. "We did one big jump for the camera right off the edge of a high dune, and it was wild—with the rear wheels clappin' each other in the air. I looked over and Faye was all bug-eyed; the back of the floorboard was scratched raw from her heels diggin' in." About another scene, McQueen said, "The thing just wouldn't turn. The throttle jammed, and we were heading right for the ocean at a terrific rate of speed. Well, on film, all you could see was this orange bug disappearing into the water. Faye came out of it soaked and smiling. Some trooper! They had to take the whole engine apart to get the saltwater out."

McQueen bought the buggy after the film was wrapped, drove it for a while, then sold it to a Meyers Manx dealer. It currently resides in Hawaii, and now belongs to an owner who wishes to remain anonymous.

Recall that in Chapter 1, we described many of Steve McQueen's most significant personal cars.

Among them was a 1967 Ferrari 275 GTS/4 NART Spyder, one of 10 built. Why did he buy that particular model? Because another one, chassis number 09437, was used in the filming of *Crown*. Life, indeed, imitates art.

Chassis 09437 is a monumentally significant automobile for several reasons. One of which is the fact that Thomas Crown didn't drive it; it belonged to Dunaway's character, Vicki Anderson (apparently, insurance investigation work paid well, at least in the movies). Another is that it was the first of the 10 NART Spyders constructed. Another still is that it is but one of two NARTs bodied in aluminum. And it lived an interesting life even before it showed up on the *Crown* set.

The NART Spyder model wasn't designed as a race car. But the GT (production-based) racing ranks in those days were still populated by cars that were driven to the track, stripped of nonessentials, raced, then driven home; 09437 was pressed into on-track duty. It was shipped to Chinetti not long after completion, and he entered it in the 12 Hours of Sebring in 1967. Although a luxury *gran turismo* convertible with a full interior, this car was reasonably well

The McCluggage/Rollo NART Spyder, Sebring 12-hour race, March 1967. This particular Ferrari enjoyed an amazing career as a racer, magazine cover model, and, of course, movie car. It is seen here wearing its original yellow paint, prior to being painted dark red for the latter two uses.
John Clinard

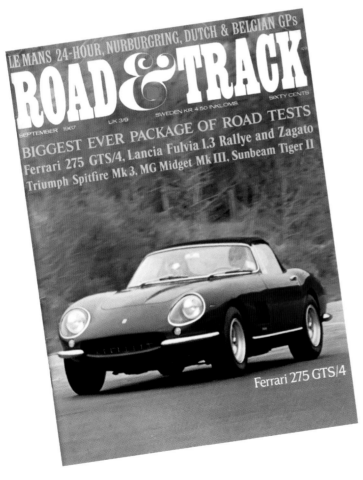

Road & Track magazine, September 1967

suited to endurance racing. Its alloy body made it lighter than other similar cars, and the race reliability demonstrated by Ferrari V-12 engines was up to the task.

Chinetti entered the Ferrari under his own North American Racing Team banner, to be driven by all-female team of Denise McCluggage and Pinkie Rollo. The car was little modified from street spec. A roll bar was added behind the seats, and the wooden trunk floor was used as a pit board. The McCluggage/Rollo entry fared well in the grueling Sebring enduro, finishing second in class and 17th overall. It's interesting that McQueen would encounter a car that raced at Sebring in this film, as he himself competed there in 1962 and 1970 (see Chapter 3).

After the race, Chinetti's shop freshened up the mechanicals and painted 09437 a deep burgundy. It was then the subject of a road test in *Road & Track* magazine. Appearing on the cover of *R & T*'s September 1967 cover, the editors summarized their impressions by proclaiming it "the most satisfying sports car in the world."

The already-accomplished Ferrari appears in *The Thomas Crown Affair* for less than 30 seconds, but it left its mark on the film in a big way by establishing Faye Dunaway's character as one who has

Ferrari NART Spyder 09347 today, having been returned to its original color. As a 1960s-era road-going machine, this rare, valuable, and sweet-driving Ferrari is a high watermark. And an expensive one. *Winston Goodfellow*

taste and wherewithal rivaling Crown's. It looks resplendent parked at the polo fields, where the seductive Miss Anderson comes face to face with Crown for the first time. Its next and final appearance is parked in front of an art auction, where Thomas Crown gives it a long, slow appraisal. Does that furtive look represent character Crown's recognition that this intriguing woman is nearby, or was Steve McQueen contemplating his next automotive purchase? Perhaps both.

Chassis 09347 was ultimately repainted its original pale yellow, and journalist/photographer Winston Goodfellow drove 09347 for *Motor Trend Classic* magazine. He wrote about "blasting around in the ultimate 1960s cool with the top down, that V-12 howl and four exhaust trumpets coming to life with any thrust on the long-travel throttle. The symphony is particularly delicious as we glide along the empty countryside freeway at a comfortable 90–100-mph clip, the supple suspension easily soaking up road imperfections. The steering is light and direct, that lovely engine melody dominating the aural experience, the view over the long hood nothing short of spectacular."

Investment banker and avid Ferrari collector Bernie Carl is the car's current owner, purchasing it for over $4,000,000 at auction in August 2005. "The 275 was the last of the Ferraris that are lithe and not too brutish, and the NART is the best of the bunch," noted Carl. "It's also luxurious enough for long, multiple-day rides and makes fantastic sounds." Summarized journalist Goodfellow, "It's no wonder the producers determined there wasn't a better car for Ms. Vicki Anderson to catch the attention of one Mr. Thomas Crown."

Bullitt (1968)

The chase scene from *Bullitt* was and remains the best ever filmed. There have been some valiant challengers: the late John Frankenheimer's heart-pounding work through the streets of Paris in *Ronin*; making Minis fly in *The Italian Job* (the original and the remake); *The Seven-Ups*, which involved some of the same folks who worked on *Bullitt*. But when the lists are made and the bets are laid down, *Bullitt* comes out on top. Every time.

In spite of a few charming continuity goofs and cameras occasionally visible in the back seat of Lieutenant Frank Bullitt's tire-smoking Mustang fastback, the scene was lauded for its authenticity and realism. See it on a big screen today, and the views out of the windshield as the Mustang and bad guys' Dodge Charger careen down San Francisco's Taylor Street will still make your stomach roll.

McQueen plays Frank Bullitt, a grizzled veteran investigator with the San Francisco Police Department. His girlfriend is the nubile Jacqueline Bisset, and the reptilian politico villain is played by Robert Vaughn at his best. I visited San Francisco in the spring of 2006 and drove most of the chase scene route, in preparation for an article in *Motor Trend Classic* magazine.

From its earliest iterations, the script called for an "automotive action scene"; this was likely one of the reasons McQueen and his Solar Productions were involved in the first place. The actor insisted on absolute realism, with no camera speedups, and of course this was long before the notion of computer-generated animation. As his production company

(see page 91) was making the film, he was in a position to make these mandates.

Ford was the official car provider for the movie, the main four-wheeled characters being two 1968 Mustang GT 390s, painted that now-famous shade of Highland Green Metallic. The cars carried back-to-back serial numbers, and although rumors persist that one was really a 302-powered car and one had an automatic trans, hard-core Bullitteers have vetted the build codes and confirm both were 325-horse, big-block, four-speed models.

Race car driver and constructor legend Max Balchowsky (of Old Yeller fame) was called upon to modify the cars for heavier-than-routine duty. Suspensions were beefed up, as were their pickup points. Koni adjustable shocks were installed, along with numerous camera mounts. The stock exhaust systems retained their small glasspack mufflers but lost

The look of Bullitt: intense blue eyes, blond hair, tweed blazer, blue turtleneck, and a Highland Green '68 Mustang GT fastback. *Warner Brothers/Photofest*

The making of this image was perfectly timed, not only showing the Charger in midair as it careened down the hill, but also the green VW that appeared in so much of the chase scene. The Bug was driven by a crew member, and since several cameras were rolling on any given take, it appears from numerous angles. *MPTV.net*

the transverse muffler in favor of straight pipes out the back, all the better to hear the thumping 390. Stories vary as to the level of engine mods. The Mustangs had manual steering and no air-conditioning.

Equally important is what the Mustangs lacked. All the badging was removed, and various chrome pieces were painted black or body color. All the chrome pieces from the grille were binned. The stock wheels were swapped for 15-inch American Racing Torq-Thrust D mags. McQueen had the stock, none-too-pretty steering wheel replaced with a 1967 Shelby piece, which Tony Nancy wrapped in leather for him. The look was menacing to say the least.

The villains' famously black 1968 Dodge Charger, manhandled about by actor/stunt driver Bill Hickman, is an equally integral plot element. Two matching Charger R/Ts were employed, equipped with 375-horsepower, single-four-barrel 440-ci Magnum V-8s and four-speed transmissions (it's possible one may have had an automatic). Although they were R/T models, the movie Chargers ran more conservative hubcap and whitewall rolling-stock combos. That's an important point because if they'd had Magnum 500 or alloy wheels, they wouldn't have been able to toss away all those hubcaps during the chase scene. The Charger's large, flat body panels, hideaway headlights, and black grille and paint job helped create the ominous look. Modifications were minimal: The torsion bars were shortened, the control arms beefed up, and police-spec rear springs were installed. But the powertrains were stock. One of the big bad Dodges was totaled in the filming of the chase's final scene, while the other also has been confirmed as destroyed.

The 10-minute-or-so chase sequence was filmed during May 1968. The crew for any given scene numbered 50 to 60, including the actors, stuntmen, and drivers, plus camera, sound, and communications people. Because of some clever editing—*Bullitt* received an Oscar for it—the scene flows seamlessly from location to location. Contrary to popular belief, the various locales are disjointed, and the chase route cannot be driven as it occurs in the film. The scene takes place primarily in the Russian Hill

The Mustang chases the Charger south out of San Francisco proper, on their way to Guadalupe Canyon Parkway. Other than the fact that there was no Transamerica building in 1968, this portion of the city's skyline hasn't changed all that much. *Warner Brothers/Photofest*

area of San Francisco and south of the city in the Guadalupe Canyon Parkway vicinity of Daly City.

Before tracing the route, I visited the corner of Clay and Taylor streets. This exact intersection isn't shown in the chase, but it's where Frank Bullitt's apartment is located. The ground-floor unit has since been converted to a garage, and he occupied the second- or third-floor apartment. Across the street is the liquor and grocery shop where Bullitt purchased an armload of frozen dinners then walked outside, gave the newspaper machine a pop with his fist, and stole a paper. "People still walk up to that paper machine and pound on it," says the store's current owner. "They still remember." A lone photo of McQueen hangs near the entrance.

Army Street, just off Highway 101, where the chase begins to form, has been renamed the ubiquitous Cesar Chavez Boulevard. The car wash seen in the film is gone, and some of the roadwork has changed the landscape. But one landmark a few miles away, Bimbo's 365 nightclub at 1025 Columbus Avenue, looks exactly as it does through the Mustang's windshield when, at roughly one hour, eight minutes, and

30 seconds into the film, stunt driver Bill Hickman fastens his seatbelt, mashes the Charger's throttle, and bangs a hard left, igniting the mayhem.

Things get interesting around the intersection of Taylor and Filbert Street. This is where the Mustang and Charger fly through the air numerous times. The hills are steep, more so than they look on screen, and the bumps abrupt. It's no wonder the cars' chassis and suspensions needed reinforcement and were checked over nightly by the crew. A broken axle, spindle, or wheel during one of these stunts would've been disastrous.

Larkin and Chestnut is where the Charger takes a turn too wide, knocking out a camera. It's also where McQueen overshoots a right turn, backs up, and then smokes the Mustang's left rear tire for all it's worth. This misstep looked and sounded so cool that even McQueen agreed it had to stay in the final film. Bullitt chases the Charger down Larkin Street, a narrow curve to the left. Alcatraz Island is clearly visible in the distance, as are portions of the Embarcadero.

The cars roar along Marina Boulevard, and it isn't long before they're on fast, semisecluded

Guadalupe Canyon Parkway, south of the city. Things get hairy here: shotgun blasts, speeds of over 100 miles per hour, and door and fender banging that would do a NASCAR race proud, prior to the chase's explosive conclusion.

There's always been a bit of speculation as to how much of the wheel work McQueen performed, but the truth is straightforward. Bud Ekins did most of the jump scenes, where the risk of the movie's star getting hurt was too great. McQueen did the shots where he was clearly visible to camera, plus much of the high-speed work near the end of the chase. Stunt coordinator Carey Loftin drove a few key scenes too.

"Carey Loftin was the stunt coordinator on *Bullitt*. He wanted me to come up to San Francisco and be one of the stunt men," recalls Ekins. "Steve started the chase scene [in the Mustang] behind Bill Hickman [in the Charger]. Hickman was a real dingbat, but he could drive, and drive well. Steve tried to follow him, and the second turn he went around, he

lost it and spun out, and damn near hit a camera. Cary said, 'Get him out of the car,' and said to me, 'Ekins, get in the clothes.' Next thing I know, I'm at the top of that big hill, following Hickman, jumping down the hills, flying through the air. Any time Hickman was in front of me, I could see the entire undercarriage of his car. If he lost it, I'd have had him.

"Steve never had any problem with being taken out of the car. When he found out that I was doubling him in the Mustang, they gave me a six a.m. call and him a ten o'clock call. One day, he showed up on the set, and I was jumping the car down the hill—in his clothes! He was very funny about all of it. He came up and said, 'Where in the hell did you learn how to drive like that?' I said, 'Back and forth to work, I guess.'

"He also said, 'You've done it to me again. Everybody thought I did that jump in *The Great Escape*.' And on one of those nighttime talk shows he had to admit that I did it. 'And now,' he said, 'whenever someone thinks I was jumping that car

Few movie stills exist from the filming of *Bullitt*. This action shot, likely snapped during the jump scenes, shows the Mustang with a side-view mirror; the other car appears identical, save for the lack of an exterior mirror. Look close, and it appears to be Bud Ekins at the wheel. *MPTV.net*

down the streets of San Francisco, and the next talk show I go on, I'm going to have to say, 'Well, no I didn't do it.' Steve didn't do any of the hard stunt-driving in the movie, although he drove it a lot of the time. Any time that you can't see his face very plainly, it's me. They'd cut back and forth between him at the wheel and me; you see a lot of the back of my head."

So, McQueen didn't do the riskiest stunts, but he did pedal for the camera. As the chase progressed south of out San Francisco, there are some high-speed sections on flat roads where there's no doubt it was McQueen at the wheel. "The level runs were as wild as the hill stuff. Here was Bill Fraker hangin' out of that stripped-down racing Chevy [a Chevy-powered racing chassis that was configured as a camera car], sittin' on a chair with his camera stuck out there at 114 miles per hour, right down the city street about six feet away from me, while I drove flat out with cement standards whippin' past us. . . "

Another intense scene involved McQueen and Ekins, Steve driving the Mustang and Bud aboard a motorcycle. McQueen recalled, "When he told us he was going to do this stunt, I really didn't want him to do it. 'You're liable to get kissed off, and your wife'll never forgive me,' I told him. But he was stubborn, convinced he could do it okay, so we let him go ahead. Man, I'll tell you, I never saw anything as scary as having him throw that BSA down in front of us. He must have slid at least seventy-five feet along the blacktop. I just twisted the Mustang sideways to miss him, spun twice, and slapped the bank—which wasn't in the script!"

The chase's final scene involved the two cars barreling down a hill, neither giving way, with the bad guys in the Charger headed straight for an elaborately rigged gas station set that was constructed specifically for this purpose. "We had Carey Loftin dressed in my jacket driving the Mustang for this end sequence," said Steve. "There's almost nothing he can't do. We had him come down the highway, side-towing the Charger. The two cars looked as if they were still racing. Then he had to work a quick-release gimmick at just the right second, sending the Dodge across the road into the gas pumps. At which point the nitro goes and we've got our scene."

It almost went wrong; in spite of Loftin's extreme skill, he either had the car pointed slightly off-angle or he released the Charger from the Mustang's grasp too soon. No matter, it actually headed off *behind* the faux station. Fortunately, an astute special effects man triggered the charges anyway. "In the film," said McQueen, "if you watch *real* close, you can see the Dodge overshoot the pumps. But it all came out fine."

One of the Mustangs was so badly damaged during filming it was judged unrepairable and scrapped. The second, chassis 8R02S125559, was sold to a Warner Brothers employee after filming was completed. He elected to sell it a few years later and advertised it in 1974 in *Road & Track* magazine. There may have been another owner or two in

Cinema Retro, a British magazine dedicated to cult films of the 1960s and 1970s, was launched in January 2005. This, its first issue, contained an interview with McQueen and another article that paid tribute to *The Great Escape*.

A rarely seen movie still of Lt. Frank Bullitt peering out of the windshield of his car. The rectangular shaped reflection at the top of the Mustang's wind wing is a large movie light, intended to light up the car and particularly its driver. *Warner Brothers/Photofest*

Not only did McQueen and Jacqueline Bisset (who played Frank Bullitt's girlfriend) make a handsome couple, but she too had great taste in cars. Here, Cathy takes Bullitt to the scene of yet another murder in her Porsche 356 Cabriolet. *Warner Brothers/Photofest*

between, but its current owner has remained anonymous since then.

Over time, other film producers, countless Mustang fans and car collectors, and even McQueen tried to purchase it—all unsuccessfully. When last seen, it showed about 66,000 miles on the odometer and had suffered minor front-end accident damage. The paint was faded and chalked, but the welded-in camera mounts were intact, and numerous holes that were drilled to accommodate other filming and lighting equipment are confirmed present. The owner reportedly plans a minimal restoration to make the car

Above: Looking respectfully close to the real thing, Dave Kunz's '68 GT fastback cruises Guadalupe Canyon Parkway, where the last high-speed section, and the final scene, of the chase took place. **Right:** The interior of Kunz's car is a bit dressier than the original *Bullitt* Mustangs. McQueen dispensed with the '68 Mustang's padded safety steering wheel, opting instead for a 1967 Shelby Mustang three-spoke wheel, with a leather rim stitched by Tony Nancy. *Evan Klein*

roadworthy yet maintain the original patina. In the meantime, having spent many years hidden in Kentucky, it now sits locked in a building in the South.

As the original was not to be had, a suitable facsimile stood in during my trip to San Francisco. Dave Kunz is a consummate car enthusiast and

Mustang lover. He bought his Highland Green 1968 Mustang GT 390 in November 1992. "It was bone stock, in clean condition, and even though it was the same model and color as the *Bullitt* movie cars, I had no initial intention of building a replica. A few

continued on page 92

SOLAR POWER

After the financial and critical success of *The Thomas Crown Affair* in 1968, Steve McQueen spread his wings and turned his Solar Productions—formed primarily as a tax shelter in 1963—into a full-scale production company.

Solar contracted with Warner Brothers-Seven Arts studio in 1967 to produce three pictures starring McQueen and a further three without the superstar. When the first movie, *Bullitt*, went almost a million dollars over budget, the six-movie deal turned into one. But Warner's loss was another studio's gain.

CBS, which wanted to get into the big screen business, formed Cinema Center Films in 1969. The new company welcomed McQueen with open arms and agreed to produce his next two pictures: *The Reivers* and *Le Mans*. Soon, Solar Productions gave birth to an offshoot called Solar Plastics Engineering.

Solar Plastics' factory was located in North Hollywood and produced support products for dune buggies and motorcycles. Some of the components included form-fitting racing seats (which McQueen helped design and patented), plastic fenders, and tool kits designed to fit underneath the seat of a motorcycle. Solar sponsored many of McQueen's racing endeavors, such as the Baja Boot off-road racers. "It was a company that was about a quarter-century ahead of its time," says Nikita Knatz, a production designer for Solar. "I can't imagine the kind of money it would make in today's automotive market."

McQueen had better success with Solar Productions, which agreed in 1969 to finance Bruce Brown's documentary, *On Any Sunday*. Its theatrical release eventually turned a $10 million profit. But the Solar dynasty came to a halt with the filming of *Le Mans*. When budget overruns forced Cinema Center Films to exercise a legal takeover of production, it was too much for McQueen, recalled Solar Vice President

SOLAR PRODUCTIONS, INC.

Robert Relyea. "The loss of control meant complete defeat to Steve," Relyea said in 2007. "It was something he couldn't live with, and it left a bad taste in his mouth."

There were also financial issues. Contrary to popular belief, Solar never went public. It was owned solely by the McQueens, and after a financial troubleshooter named Bill Maher was hired to sort things out, the company was found to be insolvent. McQueen's dream production machine—and its plastics, engineering, and racing arm—was shut down for good in 1971.

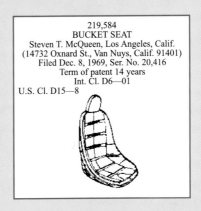

219,584
BUCKET SEAT
Steven T. McQueen, Los Angeles, Calif.
(14732 Oxnard St., Van Nuys, Calif. 91401)
Filed Dec. 8, 1969, Ser. No. 20,416
Term of patent 14 years
Int. Cl. D6—01
U.S. Cl. D15—8

"I got concerned when a friend of mine flipped his buggy and messed up his neck," said McQueen. "So I got me a big hunk of clay, had some drawings made, and worked out this seat. We called it the Baja Bucket [and it] has saved more than one life on a flip-over." This is the illustration used in patenting the Baja Bucket design. *Chad McQueen collection*

Another view that has changed remarkably little since 1968 is this look down Larkin Street. That's Alcatraz Island off in the distance. Kunz's Mustang is pointed in the direction that the chase followed down this narrow, winding street. *Matt Stone*

continued from page 90
things in my garage tumbled onto it during the 1994 Northridge earthquake, gouging the paint. My insurance company paid to have it stripped and redone. I visited the paint shop before the white C-stripes and some of the chrome trim was reinstalled. Something clicked, and before I knew it, I was looking at movie photos trying to figure out the rest of the details."

Kunz's Mustang is a faithful, but not exact, replica. It has power steering and air-conditioning. It also has a lower console and retains the chromed rear lettering, chrome taillight trim, and dual side mirrors. But other trim bits have been removed, the lower rocker trim painted body color, the grille-mounted horse emblem and driving lights pulled out, the exhaust system modified, a close replica of McQueen's favorite 1967 Shelby Mustang steering wheel installed, proper American Racing Torq-Thrust D wheels and Koni shocks bolted on, and numerous other details affected to make the car a convincing twin to the cars McQueen, Ekins, and Loftin bashed around the hills of San Francisco.

Kunz doesn't go out of his way to promote his car as an official replica, but Ford has used it a number of times in that capacity. It appeared in a 1997

TV commercial filmed for the launch of the Ford Puma and also in Sheryl Crow's music video for her 2002 song, "Steve McQueen." Ford also used the car during its launch of the 2001 Bullitt Mustang (Chapter 5).

As I gunned Kunz's Mustang through the streets of San Francisco, it must have known it was on its heritage turf. The 390 engine isn't as powerful or robust as a 427 or 428, or the Charger's 440, and it isn't a revver, either. But there's lots of torque, it pulls strongly from 2,000 to 4,500 rpm, and it sounds magnificent (turn up the volume). The factory Ford Top-Loader four-speed is a willing partner and shifts well even though it's never been rebuilt. The Koni shocks make for a firm ride, but it's still comfy enough for long freeway drives, and the A/C blows cold. Just don't expect much feel or feedback from the power steering system. Never mind, the view of San Francisco out its windshield is spectacular.

In a 1968 *Motor Trend* interview, McQueen said, "I always felt a motor racing sequence in the street, a chase in the street, could be very exciting because you have the reality objects to work with, like bouncing off a parked car. An audience digs sitting there watching somebody do something that I'm sure almost all of them would like to do."

No kidding.

The Reivers (1969)

Steve McQueen performing William Faulkner? After the super-cool characters he portrayed in *The Thomas Crown Affair* and *Bullitt*, it was likely a welcome respite for McQueen to partake in a light-hearted comedy, albeit one with a message. He did it with style, and of course, there was a car involved.

The Reivers was adapted from the Faulkner novel of the same name. It's a coming-of-age story

McQueen as Boon and the Von Dutch–built Winton Flyer replica in *The Reivers. 1978 Mel Traxel/MPTV.net*

Right: Movie cars are seldom what they seem. An original 18-horsepower Winton powerplant wasn't necessary, as it wouldn't be seen, nor did it have the power required. So Von Dutch used a BMC inline-four, as found in Minis, MGs, and many other British cars. Petersen Automotive Director Dick Messer says that "it runs great and is really pretty quick." **Below:** Von Dutch's hand-engraved brass plate shows that the car was built at his Southern California home/shop for Solar Productions in 1968. *Matt Stone*

for an 11-year-old boy named Lucius Priest. His grandfather is the patriarch of a wealthy Mississippi family and the owner of a shiny, new 1905 Winton Flyer. McQueen plays Boon Hogganbeck, a ranch hand and goodhearted troublemaker who works for Lucius' grandfather, as does Ned McCaslin, the family chauffer. Boon wants to visit his girlfriend/prostitute in Memphis and convinces young Lucius

that he should come along. They kidnap the Winton and head for the big city, only to discover Ned stowing away amongst the luggage. The triumvirate is complete, the adventure begins, and it doesn't stop until the film's final scenes.

Not many are familiar with Winton automobiles. Alexander Winton first produced bicycles in Cleveland, Ohio, in the late 1800s and is recognized

After the filming of *The Reivers* was complete, McQueen asked Von Dutch to "hang on to it for a while." The Winton Flyer was later sold, but McQueen reacquired it. He then owned it until he died, and it was sold at his 1984 estate auction. Subsequent owners restored it, and it appeared as good as new when it was again resold in 2006. *Matt Stone*

as one of the pioneers of automobile manufacture in America. He built his first motorized vehicle in 1896—using more than a few bicycle parts—and formed the Winton Motor Carriage Company in 1897. A year later, he made the first commercial sale of an automobile in the United States.

Wintons were innovative machines for their day, and the Winton Company was awarded numerous design patents. Every Winton was handmade, which caused the company to struggle as competitors like Ford Motor Company established faster, more cost-efficient assembly lines. Winton fought on until 1927, when he could no longer compete. He left the automobile business for good, although his company's kin, Electro-Motive and the Cleveland Engine Division of General Motors, continued producing stationary and locomotive powerplants until the early 1960s.

Faulkner's choice of a rare automobile suited McQueen's tastes, yet it did pose a problem: where, in the late 1960s, did one find a complete and running 1905 Winton Flyer that would be up to the rigors of film production? Nowhere. So Solar had one built. For that task, McQueen turned to his personal pinstriping and fabrication guru, Von Dutch. He "made it all himself, from the frame up," said McQueen, "out of old aluminum furnace sidings and God knows what else. When he showed it to us, we all gasped. The thing was just *beautiful*—bright yellow, gleaming with polished brass—a perfect replica of a genuine 1905 Flyer, but with a modern powerplant under the hood. We needed some kick on those Southern goat trails." True enough: It needed to be able, according to McQueen, to "ram into mudholes, slam over ditches, and drive flat out on rutted roads."

The Von Dutch Flyer appears faithful to the original . . . enough, anyway, for the movies. Underhood, in place of the Flyer's original 18-horsepower engine, is a BMC inline-four, much like the one powering millions of Minis, although mounted longitudinally and driving the rear wheels. What most impresses is the detailing of this one-of-a-kind machine, which showcases Von Dutch's do-anything fabrication capabilities. The toolbox on the driver side, the matching red, white, and blue jerry cans on the opposite flank, the brass trim, even a functioning folding top—all were either appropriated from other uses or made from scratch, by hand.

The Flyer is an important cast member, and this is apparent from the opening scene, where it arrives in town via railcar. A curious Boon is on hand to see his boss' new pride and joy, and you can see that it won't be long before he's behind the wheel—with authorization or without. Soon after Boon, Ned, and the boy head out on their big adventure, they encounter a mud hole. On the other side is a man with a horse, who makes a good living pulling out wagons and cars that get stuck in the muck. Boon proudly declares that "this is an 18-horsepower automobile" and that he has no intention of getting stuck, much less paying the scalper's outrageous $5 rescue fee. Of course, the Flyer gets buried up to its axles, the spinning wheels covering him in the glop. He pays and drives along.

An interesting bit of movie sleight-of-hand involves the starting of the engine and its sound. The BMC motor is fired via a conventional starter and sounds like a 1960s-era four-cylinder engine. An original Winton powerplant would make much more of a "puka puka" sound at idle and would be started with a hand crank at the front of the car. McQueen starts the car several times during the film, of course faking the cranking sequence. The engine sound was dubbed in.

Once in Memphis, a more-than-tipsy Ned trades the Flyer for a race horse; now, the trio is really in trouble. The only way to win it back is in a horse match race, with young Lucius as the jockey. They ultimately prevail and waste little time piloting the Flyer back to the family ranch. There's more than a little hell to pay for all of them, but once all the lessons are learned and apologies made, Boon, Ned, and Lucius find themselves back aboard the Winton.

Boon fires the engine, and the final scene shows them in the car, perhaps plotting their next big adventure—although the wheelless machine now sits on blocks, ensuring they won't be going anywhere anytime soon.

As with so many of McQueen's movie cars, Solar Productions ended up with the Von Dutch Flyer, and it was sold at the 1984 estate auction. It traveled through numerous owners in the meantime and was restored around 2000. The car that McQueen once referred to as "the *real* star of the picture" was purchased by the Petersen Automotive Museum in the fall of 2006, joining its permanent "Cars of the Stars" collection.

On Any Sunday (1971)

There's no better way to get a handle around this charming film than to let Steve McQueen set up the story himself, as he did for this movie trailer: "A few years ago, Bruce Brown made the classic film about surfing, *Endless Summer*. Now, he's made a new film about my favorite sport, motorcycle racing. It's called *On Any Sunday*. It shows, for the first time, what the sport is really like, and I'm proud to have a little ride-on in the film. It wasn't much, but it gave me a chance to work with some real stars. Whether you ride or not, I think you'll enjoy *On Any Sunday*."

Brown was born in San Francisco but grew up around the beaches of Southern California. He was into photography at an early age and began shooting the surfing scene with still and later motion picture cameras. He'd already self-produced several low-budget surfer flicks by the time he made *Endless Summer* in 1966, but it was this now-cult classic that established him as an expert documentary filmmaker. He had no formal training in the movie business, which he later declared to his advantage.

In a tribute to McQueen that Brown produced in 1991, he tells the story of how the two of them came together on the making of what could be considered the motorcycle equivalent to *Endless Summer*. "Steve was my partner making *On Any Sunday*. He provided the financing, and his company, Solar Productions, handled the business. My crew and I made the movie. A lot's been said about Steve; all I can add is that he was a fine motorcycle rider, a helluva good partner, and a nice guy. It is often overlooked how good a rider Steve was. He was a member of the International Six Days Trials team in 1964 [see

On Any Sunday's three amigos: Mert Lawwill, Malcolm Smith, and McQueen. *Cinema 5 Distributing/Photofest*

Chapter 4], a top-ranked amateur in the desert at one time, and a very good amateur motocrosser. He respected his fellow racers, and they respected him. He liked to work on his own equipment and got his knuckles bloody just like the rest of us. Steve rarely went to the Academy Awards ceremony, but when we got an award for our movie from the motorcycle industry, he was excited to go to the banquet. Steve always seemed the most relaxed sitting around, bench racing with his buddies."

Although the film covers a wide variety of motorcycle competition, it centers on three individuals: AMA national champion Mert Lawwill, the incomparable Malcolm Smith (numerous wins in the Baja 500 and 1000, plus too many other victories and championships to count), and McQueen. He isn't listed in a starring role, nor does he have a particularly large part in it, although his presence is always felt, and he appears in several scenes at different times throughout the film.

One race McQueen ran several times over the years is the Elsinore Grand Prix, held just north of San Diego, California. Brown noted, "He didn't feel very comfortable when people would recognize him, but he wasn't above using his famous face if need be. I was with him at Elsinore when he walked up to a stranger's house, knocked on the door, and asked if he could use the bathroom. And they said, 'Sure . . . Steve?' His car racing experience gives him the ability to pick the perfect line through the corners." *Sunday* covers McQueen's 1970 Elsinore run, where he finished 10th among more than 500 competitors. He is seen throughout the film most often riding his Husqvarna 400, although he ran the Elsinore race on a 250-cc Husky.

Nearly all of the footage was captured at a variety of racing venues, but the closing scenes were purpose shot. They feature Smith on a Husky 250, Lawwill on a Harley-Davidson, and McQueen, again on the 400, riding around on the beach at sunset, cavorting like three young deer running through the forest. What really strikes you is how much fun these guys were having, even if it was just hamming it up for the cameras. The smile on McQueen's face is so genuine, and even though they weren't riding particularly hard, it's clear that the actor had abilities on a motorcycle that weren't that far off from those of the two professional racers.

This long sequence at the end of the movie was shot at Camp Pendleton, a Southern California marine base. The story goes that even the resourceful Brown had no idea how to navigate through the red tape required to film a movie on a military property. McQueen volunteered to make some contacts. Once he'd found the appropriate general, the beauracracy melted away, and within days, the film crew was at work filming on the Pendleton's scenic coastline. The movie was nominated for the Academy Award for Best Documentary, although it did not win the Oscar.

McQueen's only line in *On Any Sunday* tells a lot about the film and about the man who uttered it: "Every time I start thinking the world is all bad, then I start seeing people out there having a good time on motorcycles; it makes me take another look."

Le Mans (1971)

Steve McQueen's vision was simple: Create the best, most realistic movie about motorsports ever made. It was a story that began years before filming took place during the summer of 1970, and its aftermath impacted McQueen for the rest of his life.

Le Mans was a saga that cannot be done any justice in any one chapter in a book this size. The good news is that there is a much larger volume dedicated strictly to the making of this movie, which, in spite of a less-than-stellar script, has since become acknowledged as one of the greatest racing films of all time. Racer and documentary filmmaker Michael Keyser and co-author Jonathan Williams published *A French Kiss With Death: Steve McQueen and the Making of Le Mans* in 1999. Its 460 pages cover every aspect of the movie: the people involved, the cars, and the impact on the lives of McQueen and others. If you really want the whole story, I recommend it highly. Here, we'll stick primarily to the cars involved, as that singular aspect of the story is plenty amazing.

McQueen, again teamed up with John Sturges, was chasing production of a script called *Day of the Champion*, about the highs and lows of a troubled Grand Prix driver with the F1 circus as its backdrop. McQueen was filming *The Sand Pebbles* in Taiwan at the time (1965). Director John Frankenheimer was also moving ahead with a movie called *Grand Prix*, starring McQueen's friend, neighbor, and twice costar James Garner. *Grand Prix* was running ahead of *Champion* in terms of production schedule, and the latter would have followed the Frankenheimer production in release. Warner Brothers pulled the plug on *Champion*, not wanting to follow with a second film of the same genre.

McQueen kept himself busy. His next two films, *The Thomas Crown Affair* and *Bullitt*, were among his biggest hits. But by 1969, at the height of his stardom and fully in command of Solar Productions, he was ready to make his magnum opus racing movie. Most of his racing experience took place in sports cars, and he had become enamored with the great endurance events like Sebring, the 24 Hours of Daytona, and of course, Le Mans. The latter, which has taken place in the French countryside since 1923, was the *grand dame* among them and thus the epicenter of the film.

Solar's production team attended the 1969 running of Le Mans to film the race as it happened. This was done to site the best camera locations, demonstrate to Cinema Center Films that the project was worthy, and in effect, learn how to film the movie. In a 1969 interview with *Motor Trend*, McQueen said, "For us to capture on film the greatest endurance race in the world has really got us excited. I'm thrilled because we think we'll be able to do things with the camera no one has ever done before. For instance, we'd like to effectively capture the speed of 220–225 mph at [the] Mulsanne [Straight]. If we can, cinematically, give people a pleasant feeling and yet give them the sheer sense of speed at the edge of infinity, then we've created greatness."

continued on page 104

Le MANS

1 Gulf-Porsche

20

OFF

Gulf

Steve McQueen so badly wanted to compete at Le Mans in 1970, and he even owned the car to do it. In spite of his will and passion to do so, logic prevailed, as, if he were injured, the production of *Le Mans* would have been delayed or even cancelled. Still, it's too bad, as man and machine certainly looked the part and were capable of an honest run. *National General/Photofest*

In 1970, Steve McQueen and Peter Revson drove this Porsche 908 Spyder to a Cinderella second place at the 12 Hours of Sebring race. It was re-engineered into a camera car for *Le Mans* and ran as an actual competitor. The camera shroud was probably less than aerodynamic, but it kept the camera safe and within the confines of the car, which was a concern to race officials. *Michael Keyser*

The bank of switches to the right of the steering wheel allowed the driver to turn the 908's three cameras on and off. Besides the camera in the nose, two were pointed out the back of the car, allowing for great high-speed race footage. This type of photography was revolutionary at the time, although a plan to photograph the last lap of the race went awry when the driver forgot to actuate the cameras while in front of the winning 917. *Michael Keyser*

Next page: The Solar Productions Porsche 917. *Jeffrey R. Zwart*

British actor Ronald Leigh-Hunt played the manager of the Porsche team, the role filled in real life by the ever-crafty John Wyer.
Porsche Werkphoto

continued from page 98

Ford won the 1969 running of Le Mans, its fourth consecutive victory. The Ford GT 40's competitive days were over, however, after having just beat Porsche's new 917 to the checkered flag after a history-making last-lap battle. The 1970 race was to be a battle between several better-developed 917s and Ferrari's fabulous 512s. The plan was to film the daylights out of the race, then return to Le Mans immediately after the 1970 event and stage whatever was necessary to complete the film.

McQueen's initial plan was to compete in the race himself. "Well, I don't know if I'm good enough to do Le Mans. It's awfully fast, about 160 mph average. I think we'll try to get me in Le Mans practice and see how I go. . . . Also, my dignity is at stake. I just can't have somebody powder my nose and jump up in front of 500,000 people and get into a car. We can put on some of our race ourselves, but other parts will have to have all those people. I want to see if I'm quick enough to practice for Le Mans. If I am, and, if the drivers will accept me, I'd like to run in the race."

McQueen's impressive second place at Sebring in the Solar Productions Porsche 908 only fueled this fire. After the Sebring run, the 908 was cleverly re-engineered as a camera car. One 35 mm camera was mounted under a somewhat bulbous but effective front nose piece, and two more were positioned under the rear deck, pointed aft. Control switches were mounted in the cockpit by which the driver could activate any or all of the cameras. Solar had also purchased a new Porsche 917 for McQueen to run in the race, possibly with British ace (and later F1 champion) Jackie Stewart.

The Le Mans practice meet took place in April 1970, and McQueen, the Porsches, and the production team were there. The media swarmed McQueen about the notion of him actually running the race. But the studio would have none of it. Putting its star into the race, with great risk to his safety and millions on the line, was more than it could chance. McQueen was distraught over Cinema Center putting the kibosh on this plan but struck a compromise: he could drive the 230-plus mile-per-hour Porsche for all the postrace filming. All the scenes showing McQueen in the car would at least have the realism he so craved. The 908 would be allowed to compete and film during the race, giving them the heat-of-battle footage deemed necessary to do the job.

The 917 was a beast, to say the least. Porsche family member and engineering genius Ferdinand Piech managed the car's development, leading Porsche's charge to the highest level of sports car racing. It was powered by a naturally aspirated, horizontally opposed twelve-cylinder engine mounted amidships that, in its initial 4.5-liter form, churned out about 580 horsepower. Five-liter variants had about the same horsepower, if slightly more low-end torque. The chassis was aluminum, and much of the bodywork was rendered in fiberglass. The wheelbase was a short 90.6 inches, with the driver sitting far forward in the tub. It weighed in at just 1,760 pounds, so the weight-to-power ratio was incredible. There were several body variations, designed for different needs: open or closed cockpit, *langheck* (long tail) for longer courses, or standard short tail primarily for shorter sprint races, although they ran at Le Mans as well. The 917 was rocket fast in a straight line and cornered well but was a real handful at anything over 200 miles per hour. Experienced team owner/manager John Wyer, who had so skillfully managed the 1968 and 1969 victories in the supposedly outdated Ford GT 40, switched to running factory-backed 917s for 1970.

McQueen's car, painted in the renowned Gulf Wyer Racing blue and orange livery, was christened number 20. In the race, that number would be run by Swiss F1 racer Jo Siffert and Brian Redman.

Porsche's rival for the 1970 running of Le Mans was Ferrari. No other carmaker had won at La Sarthe as many times, but Ferrari had been shuffled aside by Ford's four wins from 1966 to 1969. Maranello wanted back on top and went to Le Mans with its beautiful long-tailed 512. It was of a similar layout to the 917, although it used more aluminum in its structure. The standard 512 was of closed-coupe configuration, while the S was an open-topped car; both would run at Le Mans. The 512's 5.0-liter V-12 engine was rated at 550–575 horsepower. Each marque had already scored a major endurance win early in the 1970 season, Porsche taking the 24 Hours of Daytona while Ferrari won the 12 Hours of Sebring, in which McQueen finished second. There were four

Neile and Steve upon the family's arrival in Le Mans, summer of 1970. Behind the seemingly happy couple is the lineup of Ferrari 512s that Chad mentioned in the foreword. *Chad McQueen collection*

A young Chad McQueen cavorts among animals and 911s at Solar Village. He summarizes the experience, saying "It was one helluva summer." *Chad McQueen collection*

factory-backed 512s at Le Mans, plus seven private entries. The stage for the race, and for racing's ultimate film, was set.

Le Mans 1970 was hardly the stuff that legends are made of. Several of the 512s were out within the first three hours, so it quickly became Porsche's race to lose. And lose it would not. Porsche won Le Mans in convincing style, finishing first, second, and third; Richard Attwood and Hans Herrmann piloted the winning short-tail 917. The two remaining Ferrari 512s came home fourth and fifth. Even though none of the Wyer Gulf 917s finished, Porsche had won the race called Le Mans, and so it would win in the movie of the same name.

Of particular note was the entry that came home ninth. Le Mans requires that each car complete a certain distance to be classified a finisher, even if it was running at the end. Only seven cars met that requirement. But the Solar Productions 908, at the hands of Herbert Linge and Jonathan

Dream Garage: the three Gulf-Wyer liveried Porsche 917s used in the filming of *Le Mans*, at the garage Solar Productions rented to house all of the race and stunt cars. McQueen's character, Michael Delaney, started the race in car No. 20, and when it was totaled in an accident, was put into No. 21 to finish the race. *Courtesy Michael Keyser*

Williams, ran a clean race and, had it completed enough distance, would have finished an impressive ninth overall. The team's pit stops took much longer than the other competitors' did, because not only did the car require refueling and tire and driver changes, but the cameras needed to be swapped out for those containing fresh film. Said Williams, "[McQueen] was friendly, but I got the distinct impression he was somewhat jealous of me. I was driving his car, and I'm certain he would much rather have been a participant than a spectator." It's anyone's guess how well the 908 would have done were it running to win rather than film the race.

With the race in the books, Solar took over the Le Mans circuit for approximately four months to film the rest of the movie. The company built Solar Village as a combination garage, office complex, mess hall, and quarters for production crew, engineers and mechanics, and others. Hundreds of local extras were brought in as required. The McQueen family occupied a villa not far from the track. And in order to make the track scenes look right, Solar needed lots of race cars (which were housed in a garage in

The Ferrari 512s were just as mouthwatering as the blue and orange 917s. This photo shows another area of the garage space that housed the cars bought, borrowed, and rented by Solar to stage the racing sequences. The 512 won its share of races, although it didn't live as long or as accomplished a racing life as the 917. Perhaps that's why Porsche won the race in the film?
Courtesy Michael Keyser

Race cars, real and otherwise. While there's no doubt that the No. 22 Porsche 917 (left), the 908 coupe (right), and the sports racers in the back row were genuine race cars, the other Porsches and Corvette were dolled-up street cars. Of course, this was back in the day when GT class entrants weren't heavily modified as compared to their street-legal counterparts. So, the cheater movie cars looked and sounded credible as production-class entrants.
Paul Blancpain

Parked on a farm road just off the course, preparing for another shot, sit two 917s, the Ford GT 40 camera car, and two 512s. Talk about the ideal first few rows of a vintage race today. . . . *Peter Samuelson*

The Porschola gets ready for its big scene. While the first take with the Lolarri went awry and had to be redone, the Porschola hit its marks the first time, destroying itself in magnificent fashion. Note the crew and equipment off in the distance. *Michael Keyser*

If anything went wrong with the Porschola's performance, it was a throttle stuck wide open after its accident. Fortunately, it only had a few gallons of gas in it and nosed into a guard rail. It kept running until it burned the tire off the rim and then ran out of gas. Note the original Lola bodywork underneath the faux Porsche panels. You can even see the Lola's previous race number on the door. *John Klawitter, courtesy Michael Keyser*

the nearby village of Arnage) and a team of drivers capable of handling them at high speed in close quarters for the cameras. John Sturges was on to direct with McQueen starring as American driver Michael Delaney. An international cast filled the rest of the roles.

The roster of drivers that McQueen and Solar engaged were all top-level sports car pilots of the day: 1970 race winner Richard Attwood, Jurgen Barth, Derek Bell, Paul Blancpain, Vic Elford, Masten Gregory, 1969 Le Mans victor Jacky Ickx, Jean-

Pierre Jabouille, Gerard Larrousse, Herbert Linge, Herbert Müller, Mike Parks, David Piper, Brian Redman, Jo Siffert, Rolf Stommelen, and Jonathan Williams, to name some.

Experienced race team manager Andrew Ferguson was brought in to head the production's racing department (he'd also worked with the Solar/McQueen team at Sebring). Jo Siffert and business partner Blancpain, who owned a Porsche dealership and had solid connections throughout Europe, took on the task of procuring the cars.

Left: Some very clever camera rigging, courtesy of production designer Nikita Knatz, camera equipment whiz Gaylin Schultz, and several other members of the Solar team allowed some of the most innovative camera angles captured up until that time—long before the notion of computer-generated animation. This particular mount allowed the camera to swing out and follow a car as it was passing this 917, although driver Derek Bell said there was considerable aerodynamic interference when the camera flipped out to the side of the car at 200-plus miles per hour. *Nigel Snowdon* **Right:** Stripped-down Lolas were used to execute crash scenes, one each for a Ferrari 512 (nicknamed the "Lolarri") and Porsche 917 (the "Porschola"). The special effects team built a driver's chair that had pedals and a steering wheel, so the driver could control the car from a distance. The cars were equipped with servo motors attached to the various controls; the steering wheel was operated via a chain drive around the steering column. *Lee Katzin, courtesy Michael Keyser*

According to *French Kiss*, they purchased four Porsche 911s, a Porsche 914, two Chevron B19 sports racers, and a Corvette. All but the Chevrons were street cars converted to look like racing machines. They also bought another 917 from Porsche, less engine and transmission, the latter of which Siffert borrowed from the factory. Siffert's own 908 made a brief appearance early in the film. Siffert and company charged Solar $5,000 a week for use of these machines, including mechanics and support.

Driver David Piper leased himself and his own No. 18 Porsche 917 and a green Lola T70 to the production. Part of his deal included the sacrifice of another Lola, an older model destined for destruction in one of the crash sequences. Four Ferrari 512s were used in the production—two from a Swiss team called Scuderia Filipinetti, another from Belgian team owner Jacques Swaters, and another from Luigi Chinetti's North American Racing Team. Autodelta, the Alfa Romeo factory team, leased Solar a T33, and Matra provided a screaming, V-12-

powered Matra 650. These cars ran in addition to the 917s owned by Solar (No. 20) and Siffert (No. 21), and a third loaned to the production by John Wyer (No. 22). Porsche loaned its No. 25 long-tail 917 for two weeks, and a couple more Lolas were leased from a privateer. Today, this heady group—25 cars, give or take—would make up a spectacular vintage racing field.

Besides all of the authentic race cars required for the production, there were other vehicles and equipment needed to facilitate filming. In addition to the 908 camera car, Solar purchased a now obsolete Ford GT 40 and converted it into a cut-down, roadster configuration. This car mounted two full-sized 35 mm cameras in its nose and had provisions in the cockpit for a passenger/cameraman to ride along to operate another camera mounted on the left door. A platform was mounted on the rear deck, just aft of the driver, for a rotating Arriflex camera. Most of the conversion work was done by Gaylin Schultz, a Hollywood camera technician known for

The Ford GT 40 camera car. It did not compete in the 1970 race but did make a few passes down the pit lane to record pre-race action. It was used heavily in postrace filming, as it had room for a driver and a cameraman, allowed a wide variety of camera mounts, plus carried the rotating Arriflex camera on its rear deck. *Courtesy Michael Keyser*

The No. 22 Porsche 917 wears a camera rig as it films itself and McQueen in the No. 20 car. This shot was taken on the famous Mulsanne Straight, with the Restaurant Des 24 Heures in the background. Back in the day, this was considered one of the prime spots for watching the race, with tables often booked a year in advance. *Nigel Snowdon*

McQueen sights up a shot from the Ford camera car looking back at the 917. Note the "Solar Productions" logo stickers the GT 40 wears just below the camera. *Peter Samuelson*

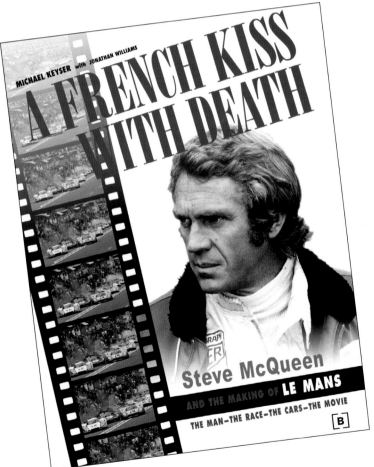

For those who want the entire saga of *Le Mans*. *Bentley Publishers*

fabricating specialized camera rigging. A variety of camera rigs and mounts were fabricated for use on the 917s and 512s, as required.

As noted, the making of the movie was a saga worthy of its own book, Keyser's *French Kiss*. Once the facility, cars, drivers, crew, and equipment were assembled, filming began—without so much as a script. While the innovative camera techniques and realistic action sequences made for arguably the best racing footage ever captured, it came at great cost. Director John Sturges quit midproduction, to be replaced by accomplished television director Lee Katzin. Driver David Piper lost his leg and totaled his 917 in an accident during filming. Delays and massive cost overruns forced Cinema Center Films to take over the management of the production, which of course angered McQueen. Meanwhile, his marriage to Neile was crumbling and would soon end in their divorce. The whole affair soured McQueen a bit on racing, as he considerably curtailed his own motorsport activity.

In spite of all this drama, *Le Mans* was completed, and its premier was held at the Indianapolis Motor Speedway the night before the Indy 500 in May 1971. It stands as one of McQueen's most notable films. *Le Mans* and *Grand Prix* are considered the greatest motor racing films made to date. Both have considerable motorsport followings, even now, and no car freak's DVD library would be complete without them.

In a 2001 documentary called *Filming at Speed: The Making of the Movie Le Mans*, which was hosted and co-executive produced by Chad McQueen, five-time Le Mans winner Derek Bell summarized his feelings about the experience: "It's stood the test of time. It's something I never thought would ever stand up thirty years later. It's like a vintage wine: better today than it was then."

continued on page 117

THE LE MANS 911
At the wheel of movie history

For its first three minutes and 40 seconds, the star of *Le Mans* isn't Steve McQueen. It's a Slate Gray 1970 Porsche 911S. It opens the film in convincing fashion, and the tranquil images of McQueen driving it through the French countryside are in stark contrast to the racing action that would follow.

McQueen had a similar 911 at home (same model and color, just a year older), but it was likely easier to acquire another car in Europe than ship his own twice across the Atlantic. Perhaps Porsche, who was involved in the production of *Le Mans*, wanted him driving the latest model. No matter, the car seen in the opening sequence, and in a few other shots, was invoiced to Solar Productions on June 1, 1970. It was a more heavily optioned car than McQueen's own, including factory-installed air-conditioning, tinted glass, a Blaupunkt Frankfurt radio, the Comfort Group (which includes leather upholstery and other interior upgrades), and front fog lamps with the then-required-in-France yellow lenses.

According to a letter from Porsche, "The car was driven as is directly to Le Mans by our people, for use by Steve and the Solar Production crew. At a later date, the car was returned to our repair shop for modifications," which included the installation of a limited-slip differential and revised gear ratios.

After its starring role in McQueen's motorsport magnum opus, the car was shipped home to Los Angeles in January 1971. McQueen elected to sell this one, instead of his '69. There is no clear reason why he chose one over the other, but one theory is that he already had installed an upgraded stereo in his first car. The '70 was advertised in the *Los Angeles Times* and was purchased by an L.A. attorney. He kept the car, largely in secret, for more than three decades. It was then purchased by another So Cal resident, Jesse Rodriquez, in April 2005.

Other than one repaint in the factory color, reupholstered front seats, new shocks, and a fresh windshield, it is completely original. It is likely the

Left: For all the great race cars in *Le Mans*, this 1970 Porsche 911S, which McQueen used as his personal car during filming and which appeared in the opening scenes of the movie, is as iconic as any of them. Here the car is parked along pit lane, with Chad in the passenger seat. *Nigel Snowdon* **Right:** The same Porsche, this time with Neile aboard, and McQueen at his 1970s mod-ish best. *Porsche Werkphoto*

amber fog lamp lenses were replaced with clear ones when the 911 was brought into the United States all those years ago. When these photos were taken, the odometer read just under 115,000 original miles, and the *Le Mans* 911S has never suffered any rust or accident damage; a wonderful example of preservation versus restoration.

Driving this car was like piloting a time machine that took me back to what it must have been like during that summer of 1970 in France. It gives off all the correct early 911 vibes, although McQueen's '69 felt faster, in spite of being a 2.0-liter versus the 1970's 2.2. After bidding the car farewell, I couldn't get home fast enough to watch the opening scenes of *Le Mans* for the umpteenth time—but with an entirely different appreciation of what it all meant.

Right: The Le Mans 911S today, living well in Southern California, as owned by Jesse Rodriguez. *Matt Stone*
Below: While the Momo Prototipo steering wheel is a period-correct piece, Chad does not believe it was present during the filming of *Le Mans* or while the car was in France. Other than the reupholstered front seats, the interior is unrestored and in fine condition. *Matt Stone*

Above: Invoice from the Porsche factory to Solar Productions. The serial numbers have been removed to prevent someone trying to clone the car, but this author has seen the original documentation, and there is no doubt that this is the Le Mans 911S. **Left:** These graphics tell the whole story: Porsche's "2.2-liter" flat six sticker in the back window, the gold "911S" badging, and the license plate "DU MANS." *Matt Stone*

continued from page 112

The Hunter (1980)

Alas, Steve McQueen's final film appearance. The film, a mostly low-key adventure romp, opened August 1, 1980, just three months prior to his passing. McQueen was already feeling the effects of the rare lung cancer that was killing him, and he was said to be extra tired at the end of a day's filming. Yet he looked terrific and moved as well as ever. Some felt his swan song should have been a production of grander scale. Yet, the main character, bounty hunter Ralph "Papa" Thorson, was someone McQueen easily identified with at the time: older and a little tired of the game, perhaps but still having what it took. And there was a lot of car play built into the script.

The movie opens with Thorson attempting to park his pale yellow '51 Chevrolet convertible.

With straight-six power and a three-on-the-tree gearshift, McQueen was capable of piloting the old Chevy as smoothly or as quickly as he wished. But the character was a far less capable driver than the actor. Thorson grinds the gears as he rolls down the street. He parks more by sound than by touch, backing the car into an onlooker's Cadillac, leaving the scene without much notice or apology. There's another amusing scene shot with the convertible's top up that underscores his relationship with the car. As he's talking to a captured prisoner inside, a piece of convertible-top trim droops. Without breaking stride, he punches the rubber molding back into place. It falls. He pushes it back up. It falls yet again. The gag never inhibits the conversation or purpose of the scene but only adds to it.

While traveling to capture another pair of prisoners, Thorson is assigned a new 1979 Pontiac

Thorson's '51 Chevy convertible, as advertised in the 1984 McQueen estate auction. As with many of his movie cars, McQueen ended up with it when filming was completed. In spite of the character's ham-fisted treatment of the shifter and clutch, and his "parking by Braille" driving style, the light yellow ragtop appeared no worse for wear.

LOT 623 1951 Chevrolet convertible.
Good running condition. Believed
to be used in 1980 movie THE HUNTER

McQueen as Ralph "Papa" Thorson, looking tough in his rented Pontiac Trans Am in *The Hunter*. Dave Friedman

Trans Am as his rental car. He begs for something older and lower key but resigns himself to the Pontiac. Papa drops the car into gear, herking, jerking, and finally burning rubber as he leaves the rental lot. He drives to a backwoods farm and gets out to search for his quarry, who promptly jump into the Trans Am. They take off, with Thorson in pursuit at the wheel of a large Massey-Ferguson harvester. The black-and-gold Pontiac and this massive tractor chase each other through tall cornfields, the bad guys throwing lighted sticks of dynamite out the window. Although the Trans Am should be able to run away from the tractor with ease, Thorson doubles back on the dimwitted brothers. They're forced into a hasty retreat and run over their own

dynamite. The scene ends with the bounty in handcuffs; the shredded Pontiac is returned to the rental counter on a trailer, its powertrain well separated from what's left of the body.

There's another chase scene involving Thorson running down a bail-busting prisoner. After a heart-stopping action sequence on a commuter train in Chicago, the bad guy runs into a parking garage and steals a Pontiac Grand Prix. Thorson commandeers a tow truck, but not before smashing into a half dozen parked cars, then scraping up yet another Cadillac in front of its owner. Thorson looks at the gent somewhat apologetically—McQueen flashes some great facial expressions here—then sets off in pursuit. Thorson and the bad guy chase each other around the multistory parking structure until they collide, which forces the pursuee's Pontiac out of the open side of the building and into the river, a dozen floors below.

Even the film's wrap-up scene works in a car as a plot element. Thorson's girlfriend is pregnant, and a life-threatening tussle with yet another bad guy puts her into labor. McQueen drives her to the hos-

pital in the Chevy. It wasn't *Bullitt*, but he was pedaling the old convertible as fast as it would go, running red lights and sliding through intersections. They make it, but barely; she gives birth to the baby *in the car*. The doctor hands Thorson his new child. He smiles. It was Steve McQueen's last big-screen moment.

Fade to black.

That same poor Pontiac met a spectacular end; luckily, Thorson wasn't aboard. *Dave Friedman*

Chapter 3
McQUEEN ON TRACK

"I'm not sure whether I'm an actor who races or a racer who acts."

—Steve McQueen, as told to biographer William F. Nolan

Steve McQueen won the first amateur sports car race he

entered. Does that surprise you? Given his competitive nature, personal drive, and all-around physical capability, it shouldn't.

McQueen had already done his fair share of racing before he ever showed up at the Sports Car Club of America race in Santa Barbara, California, that May 1959 weekend. He'd match-raced against other motorcyclists back in New York. He'd probably taken on a few other New Yorkers in his MG. But Steve McQueen and the Southern California sports car scene went together like gasoline and a match: flames were unavoidable.

His first weapon in the sports car wars was his 1958 Porsche Speedster 1600 Super, described in Chapter 1. This was a perfect starter race car for several reasons. The relatively lightweight Speedster model, with its spare interior, lack of top and windows, and cut-down windshield, was already a proven winner in SCCA competition. It was quick but not so quick

Opposite page, top: There were no full-faced helmets back in 1959, only a bowl-style lid and a pair of aviator-style goggles for protection. It's a good thing too, otherwise we wouldn't have seen that marvelous profile of a young Steve McQueen cutting his teeth as an amateur sports car racer.

Opposite page, bottom: McQueen and the Speedster at Riverside International Raceway. Riverside had just been constructed and quickly became the hub of sports car racing in Southern California. He was hard on the gas at this point; note the rear end squat and front end lift. *Chad McQueen collection*

Ronnie Bucknam, who ultimately became a professional sports car racer, follows McQueen in his own Porsche Speedster. This at an open track day at Riverside Raceway in 1959, as McQueen was being photographed for a magazine article. He enjoyed good success with the Speedster, but it wasn't long before he was ready for something faster and more sophisticated. *Chad McQueen collection*

that he couldn't handle it while learning race craft. And he already owned it.

"I was put into a novice race," McQueen said. "We had a real mixture of cars, big and small, and I had no idea where I'd finish. . . . I remember storming off the line like mad, passing a lot of other Porsches and some Triumphs, not paying much attention to my revs—until about four laps into the race, I suddenly found myself leading the field. Which shook me. Here I was skidding around the circuit between cars, going as deep into the turn as possible before braking, on the ragged edge all the way, and I thought, 'Man, what are you *doing* out there?' But I hung on and won. After that, I was hooked. Winning gives you a very heady feeling." He enjoyed more of it at SCCA races run at Willow Springs, near Palmdale, California, and at the Del Mar circuit, just north of downtown San Diego. It wasn't yet big-time motorsport, but three wins out of three events entered is a good start for anyone at anything.

Understand that McQueen's TV and movie career was really heating up about this time, so he could only race sporadically. This conflict surfaced many more times throughout the next dozen or so years. But, as he said above, he'd succumbed to the euphoria of winning. "Racing was giving me a fresh identity," he later told biographer Nolan. "I was no longer just an actor; I was a man who raced, and that was important to me—to have this separate identity."

McQueen also drove the Porsche at Riverside International Raceway at an open track day for a photo shoot. But like any rider who ultimately wants a quicker horse, McQueen was ready for a faster car before long. He replaced the Porsche with a Lotus XI in the summer of 1959. This Lotus (also referred to as a Lotus Eleven, or a Lotus 11) was produced from 1956 through 1958. It was a state-of-the-art small-bore sports racer at the time and a step up from even a capable sports car like the Speedster. The XI was

"Faster and more sophisticated" came in the form of this Lotus XI sports racer. In this car, McQueen felt he developed his driving skills from lucky weekend amateur to legitimate racer. These photos were likely taken at an SCCA meet in Del Mar, California. *Chad McQueen collection*

McQueen dices with Frank Monise in another Lotus, Santa Barbara, California. It wasn't a particularly successful weekend, as he spun the car in one event and accidentally shut off his fuel supply in another. *Chad McQueen collection*

powered by an 1,100-cc Coventry Climax four-cylinder engine, and in capable hands, the light-weight Lotus was more than a match for many 1,500-cc-class cars. "In that Lotus, I really started to become competitive. I was smoother, more relaxed; the rough edges had been knocked off my driving. I was beginning to find out what real sports car racing was all about."

His first outing in the new car took place at Santa Barbara—the site of that all-important first checkered flag just a few months earlier—over Labor Day Weekend in 1959. In the Saturday race, he dueled with another Lotus 11, finishing less than a foot behind him for a credible second place. In the main event on Sunday, he was battling the same driver, but pushed a bit too hard and spun out, killing the engine, which he admitted was his error. By then, two cars had slipped by, and McQueen had to settle for fourth. His last event in 1959 was back at Del Mar, which resulted in another DNF. "I was leading," he said, "when I accidentally hit this switch on the dash which cut my power. It was an emergency fuel

switch for changing tanks. As a result, the car just died on me. I was embarrassed about that, but I was still learning. Each time you race, you learn more."

The actor/racer conflict reared its head big-time in 1960. His TV series, *Wanted: Dead or Alive*, was a top-rated show, and he also filmed *The Magnificent Seven* with an impressive ensemble cast. The studio was more than a little concerned about McQueen's dangerous pastime and insisted he quit racing. There was no reason to keep his recently acquired Lotus. So, assuredly against his heart, he sold it. He told a reporter, "I'm cool, man. I can afford to quit racing for a while."

"A while" wasn't all that long, because *Wanted: Dead or Alive* wound down about six months later. That meant McQueen was not only free to pursue the big movie roles he was so ready for but was free of the TV producers' worries over his speed habits. The Lotus was gone, but it didn't take him long to find other ways to get behind the wheel.

McQueen signed on to act in *The War Lover*, to be filmed in England in 1961. The producers had instructed him not to race cars during filming, but this wasn't the first or last time that a warning failed to keep Steve McQueen from doing it anyway. He begged, borrowed, and (likely) bought rides at local sports car races during the weekend. According to biographer Nolan, he earned a fifth at Oulton Park, didn't fare so well at Aintree, and took a well-deserved third place at an event at Brands Hatch. At least two of these drives took place in a privately owned Mini Cooper, which may have been the impetus to purchase his Cooper S (see Chapter 1) a few years later.

An accident, also at Brands Hatch, nearly put McQueen in the cooler with *Lover*'s producers. He was running a borrowed Mini Cooper in a wet race, when one of the brakes locked up and sent him spinning sideways. A contemporary race report described the moment: "As he hurtled downhill, off the road, McQueen did a superb job of propelling the Cooper between poles and metal signs that could have demolished it. He controlled the slide until the final instant, looped, and slammed the car at an angle into a dirt embankment. The Cooper snapped around like a top, whirling and bouncing, but miraculously did not turn over." He escaped with a cut lip.

It was also while working on this film, and racing his way through the local sports car track scene, that he met British driving ace Stirling Moss. Though never a world driving champion, Moss was one of the best until an accident forced his retirement. Moss and McQueen were said to have gotten along like brothers, and the Mille Miglia sports car race winner coached the American actor on his driving.

"He was keen on cars and a very competent driver," recalls Moss. "I would rate him as a good number two, perhaps a strong number three driver. On a good day, he would have finished on the rostrum. It's hard to say what he would have become if he had gone into it professionally, because people change when they're at something full time. He would have been pretty good, though. It would have been an awful waste in the end, however, because he was too good at what he did. If he had chosen racing, sports cars and endurance racing would have been his forte. I don't think he would have made the grade

If there were a text bubble over Ken Miles' head, it would say something like, "No, Steve, not that. Look where I'm pointing." Miles went on to enjoy a spectacular racing career, mostly with Shelby American. He won the 24 Hours of Daytona and the Sebring 12-hour race with Lloyd Ruby in a Ford GT 40 in 1965, and died in a practice crash in a Ford racing prototype at Riverside in 1966. McQueen's driving suit sported both Porsche and Lotus patches, and given the hangar in the background, it's likely this happy snap was taken at Santa Barbara in 1959 or 1960. *Chad McQueen collection*

to Formula 1; it was too restrictive, and I think he rather enjoyed many other aspects of his life. But he became a top actor, so he made the right decision."

Moss also opened the door to the John Cooper racing team for McQueen, as the actor had sold his Lotus and was in search of another, even more committed race car. The Cooper T52 Formula Junior (FJ) was the first, and only, open-wheel racer Steve McQueen competed in. Powered by 1.0-liter and 1.1-liter overhead-valve BMC engines, not so different from those powering road-going Minis all over the world, the Cooper FJ was, like the Lotus, a competitive machine in the early 1960s. Racing greats such as Jimmy Clark, John Surtees, and

His TV series, *Wanted: Dead or Alive*, had wrapped, so the TV studio's mandate of "no more racing" was no longer valid. McQueen bought another race car, this Cooper T52 Formula Junior, and hit the Southern California sports car circuit again in 1962. This photo was taken at Del Mar in April 1962. *Dave Friedman*

The picture of concentration: McQueen aboard his Cooper FJ, at Cotati Raceway, 1962. *Chad McQueen collection*

Denny Hulme all drove them at some point. McQueen brought the car back to California with him (along with a Land Rover) when filming of *The War Lover* was completed.

As he was preparing to return from Europe, an interesting drive presented itself. It was March 1962, and McQueen was offered his first professional ride as a factory team driver. Through his relationship with Stirling Moss and John Cooper, he was invited to participate in the 12 Hours of Sebring endurance races in Florida as a member of the BMC team, which was run by Cooper. As you'll see, it wasn't the

last time the historic Sebring circuit figured heavily in the racing endeavors of Steve McQueen.

He competed in two separate events that weekend. "They had a kind of warm-up race there on Saturday, a three-hour production go in which all of us BMC drivers were put into Austin-Healey Sprites," McQueen said. It was raining that day, which some drivers don't enjoy, and others thrive upon.

Sebring is a complicated course, because it has several sections that are wide and fast, while others are narrow and technical. The track's surface is bumpy, which has caused many accidents and equipment damage over the years. McQueen's BMC teammates—no less than Moss, Pedro Rodriquez, and Innes Ireland—were also in the race. In spite of odds that appeared stacked against him, McQueen drove quick and smart, keeping himself and the pint-sized Healey in the hunt and out of trouble. He finished a credible ninth place out of 28 starters; none too shabby for his first experience at this course, in the wet and against more experienced drivers.

McQueen's teammate for Sunday's 12-hour main event was John Colgate of the Colgate toothpaste family, and they raced another Austin-Healey, although this car wore aerodynamic Le Mans fastback coupe bodywork and was more highly tuned than the relatively stock Sprite he drove in Saturday's three-hour race. Other than a potentially close call (McQueen was downshifting gears when the shift knob came off in his hand, causing a lurid slide from which he luckily recovered), the Colgate/McQueen

Above: Even in a crowd, whose face shines out? At the Stardust 7-11 drivers meeting, McQueen chats with another racer to his right, while a bored-looking Bud Ekins leans against the rail and stares into space. It's easy to understand, because as an experienced off-roader, Ekins had heard it all before. Motor Trend *archive*

Left: A rare photo of both Baja Boots together. Note the Solar Plastics Engineering logo on the side and nose. Motor Trend *archive*

was the darndest thing," McQueen said. "We were really battin' along, feeling good about the car and our chances with it, when we see this big fat wheel rolling along beside us. It's *our* wheel! The axle had popped. Well, that did it. We sat on our tails in the desert till help came." Interestingly enough, another nonfinisher in the same event was McQueen's pal and several times costar James Garner, who had taken a liking to off-road racing, and had proven during the filming of *Grand Prix* that he was a more-than-capable driver.

What became known as the Baja 1000 was first run in 1967, and McQueen entered the repaired and updated Boot in that race's third running, which began on October 29, 1969. Garner was back too, in a highly modified Oldsmobile Cutlass. McQueen did a prerun in his Chevy-powered Jeep in order to help get his mind around the approximately 832-mile course. The event started in Ensenada, ran the length of the Baja Peninsula, and finished in La Paz.

McQueen never intended to race at Ascot Raceway in Gardena, California, but once the word was out that he would, he decided to show up and give it a try. He ran there often during the summer of 1969, and won several times, as shown in this trophy shot. Motor Trend *archive*

Nearly 250 assorted vehicles were entered. McQueen's co-pilot that time out was Harold Daigh.

The Boot was running well. "In the fast sections," McQueen said, "it was not unusual for us to get airborne for fifty to seventy feet over road dips. The Boot rides so smooth you can overdo things. Even in bad, choppy sections it'll do sixty or so, and if you slam into a big rock at that speed you can crack an axle, or worse."

McQueen thundered ahead, chasing the win, and, no doubt, Garner. His machine, and his luck, held out not quite a third of the way through the race. After refilling a leaking cooling system, he suffered the failure of a small transmission part. Once again, all McQueen could do was park the Boot and wait for help. His Baja attempt was done, and he and Daigh were classified as nonfinishers.

There were several more off-road races on McQueen's calendar that took place in between the 7-11 and the Baja, but they were different by way of venue. Ascot Park in Gardena, California, was an historic dirt oval and most often the home of sprint car races. Ascot had also begun hosting off-road races, and Steve and Chad took one in on an August night. The whole notion was unusual, as off-road racing up until that time had taken place in the expanse of the desert, not on small, closed courses like Ascot (although Mickey Thompson would later make stadium racing a popular and successful sport).

McQueen's participation was launched out of a rumor. He said the action was "as far out as anything I'd seen in racing." A friend let him take his machine around the course. "I had myself a real bash. It was nothing but great." And that was that. Just a little practice run. Or so he thought.

The next day, a reporter contacted McQueen for an interview, as word was spreading that he intended to compete at Ascot the following weekend. "I'd never really competed on a dirt track, and I knew I could get bent way out of shape doing those crazy jumps and all. But I thought, well, the people want to see me, so why not give it a shot."

The Baja Boot was way too much truck for this compact course, so he raced a custom-built Jeepster at Ascot, also with Chevy power, like the Jeep CJ he kept at the family home in Palm Springs

Determined to turn the stillborn *Day of the Champion* project into the world's most realistic racing movie, *Le Mans*, McQueen got serious again about his driving. Solar Productions purchased this Porsche 908 Spyder, and McQueen ran it in three races as a lead up to the 12 Hours of Sebring in March 1970. This photo was taken at Holtville near San Diego, where McQueen won handily. *Porsche Werkphoto*

(Chapter 1, page 51). "It handled real good in the dirt," he said, "and was much faster than I figured. I did well enough that first night to want more. In fact, I began competing at Ascot on a fairly regular basis that summer."

In between his off-road racing activities in 1969, McQueen and Solar's production team attended the 24 Hours of Le Mans in preparation for the filming of the movie. Unlike *Bullitt*, McQueen fully intended to do all of his own driving for the cameras. Although a Gulf-Wyer–entered Ford GT 40 won the 24-hour race that year, it was clear that Porsche was knocking at the gate and would soon dominate the event. Solar purchased the Porsche 908 Spyder, which was driven in the 1969 Le Mans race by Brian Redman and Jo Siffert. "I needed to familiarize myself with a car like the 908 in order to drive there with any kind of authentic feel for the course," McQueen said. "In most Hollywood movies, the star is doubled, but I don't want any doubles for me at Le Mans. If I can't cut it in the 908 then there's no point in making the film."

With the exception of a Lola T70 Can-Am-style racer he'd once borrowed to learn the tricks of the Riverside International Raceway course, the 908 was, by far, the most serious racing machine McQueen had driven to date. Its 3.0-liter flat eight was good for about 350 horsepower. This may not sound like a lot, but in an open sports racer that weighs just 1,400 or so pounds, it made for a seriously fast ride. This particular example wore slightly longer than normal rear bodywork, and the 908 model's fishlike visage earned it the nickname "Flounder." Setting up and caring for this class of race car is well beyond the scope of most backyard mechanics, so McQueen hired Richie Ginther to look after the 908 and support him at the races. Ginther, a Formula 1 winner and a superb sports car racer, had by then retired and was proving his skills as a capable team manager.

The plan was to run the car in a few local SCCA races to get McQueen's reflexes used to modern-day endurance racers. His first outing with the now all-white 908 was at Holtville, a rough and tumble club racing course near San Diego, in February 1970. The Porsche was by far the class of the field, McQueen winning easily and setting a new course record in the process. The Solar team's next stop was a

Above: McQueen at the
wheel of the Solar
Productions Porsche 908,
1970. *Richard George*

Right: Neile did her best to
support McQueen's
endeavors but admitted to
biographer William Nolan
that "racing was a world of
Steve's I could never really
enter." Suffice it to say that
son Chad was a bit more
enthusiastic about the
whole thing. He later drove
this same car at Daytona,
29 years later. Daughter
Terry is on the right.
*Richard George, courtesy
Michael Keyser*

McQueen and the Solar 908 lead others at Riverside, 1970. The transmission failed, causing a near-disastrous spin. But all was repaired in time for Sebring. *Porsche Werkphoto*

weekender at Riverside, a much faster course. The Porsche won a preliminary race on Saturday, setting a blistering pace. Sunday didn't go as well.

"We were running Le Mans gears," he said, "because of the long straight, which gave us a top speed of 160 in fourth. I'd cleared turn nine and had shifted from third into fourth again on the pit straight, lining up for turn one, which was blind and fairly swift. I was into the turn at about 150 when the whole gearbox exploded under me! I began to slide wildly across the track, from one side to the other, using up all the road. It was real nip-and-tuck there for a while, and I didn't know if I'd come out in one piece."

After a new transmission was installed, McQueen ran one more race as a run up to Sebring in March. It was in Phoenix, where he swept the field. He was by then leading the A Sports Racer category in the SCCA's Southern Pacific region, and had he been able to continue in the series, he might have been able to earn the amateur racing title (As an aside, Chad won the SCCA National championship in the C Sports Racer class 31 years later).

The first thing McQueen had to do upon arrival at Sebring was figure out how to race with a broken foot, injured in the Elsinore Grand Prix motorcycle race a few weeks before. His crew built up a cover out of leather, metal, and duct tape that slipped over McQueen's driving shoe. *Bill Warner*

A magnificent pan blur photo of McQueen at speed, Sebring, 1970.
Harry Hurst

But given the summer's filming schedule, it wasn't in the plan. Competing in the 12 Hours of Sebring wasn't in the plan when McQueen purchased the 908 either, but he wanted to get firsthand exposure to the trials and tribulations of long-distance events.

One wouldn't think that a motorcycle race would figure into McQueen's run at Sebring, but it did. In a major way. The Elsinore Grand Prix was an annual through-the-town-and-across-the-desert race that McQueen had ridden in several times and enjoyed. So, after winning with the 908 at Phoenix, he got back on two wheels for the Elsinore. It might have been better if he hadn't.

Aboard his Husqvarna, McQueen was "coming out of a wash under a bridge with this road dip ahead, and I just kinda took one of those big jumps where you're sure you're gonna make it but you don't. And I didn't. My bike nosed into the dip, which was, like, deep—and I went ass-over-the-bars into the crowd. Didn't hurt anybody but me. My left foot was busted in six places." It surprised no one that he gathered himself up, got back on his bike, and finished the race in the top ten. But McQueen needed that left foot to operate the 908's clutch, and Sebring was just two weeks away.

The first thing he had to accomplish upon his arrival in Florida was to convince the race officials that he was capable of safely driving the car. His mechanics fashioned a boot out of leather that was designed to slip over his plaster cast. This was just one of the many factors that caused those officials, the other racers—many of whom were full-time pros with factory teams—the media, and the public to view McQueen's entry into the race with a jaundiced eye. What was an injured actor doing in a big-time professional sports car race? "I had a lot to prove out there," he said. "In a way, it was the most important race of my life."

One of his best decisions was hiring Peter Revson as his co-driver. Heir to the Revlon cosmetics fortune and, like McQueen, movie star handsome, Revson was a big-game racing driver. He'd driven Indy-type open wheelers, Formula racers, Trans-Am, you name it.

The 3.0-liter Porsche had little hope for an overall win; that honor would surely go to the factory entries from Porsche, Ferrari, and Alfa that were running in the faster 5.0-liter class. But it would be a good experience in advance of filming *Le Mans*, and if McQueen and Revson drove smart and the car

held together, they stood a good chance of finishing well in the 3.0-liter category.

Mario Andretti, teamed with Italian sports car ace Arturo Merzario, started from pole in a Ferrari 512S. The brilliant red Ferrari dominated the race from the start. Attrition is a dominating factor in endurance racing; as they say, "in order to finish first, you first must finish." Several cars in the 3.0-liter class dropped out, and the Solar 908 climbed steadily up the leader board. McQueen was five to six seconds a lap slower than his professional, and uninjured, teammate, but they drove consistently, and their pit stops were error free. More fallouts occurred, and by the 10th hour, the McQueen/Revson entry was running first in class and an amazing third overall, following only the Italian stallions in their Ferrari and the factory Porsche 917 of Pedro Rodriquez and Jo Siffert. But McQueen was hurting.

"The pain from my left leg was really getting bad," he said. "The cast had split, and I didn't know if I could keep going, but I didn't want to hand over to Pete unless I'd done my full two hours. Still, the pain was messing up my concentration. In a race, particularly a long endurance race such as Sebring, concentration is everything. You can't let your mind wander, because that's how crashes happen." Revson took over in the hopes of preserving a class win. And that's when the drama began in earnest.

Earlier in the race, the Jacky Ickx/Peter Schetty Ferrari 512S dropped out due to bearing failures in the differential. With less than two hours to go, with Merzario at the wheel, the Ferrari that had so dominated the race thus far succumbed to the same fault. Teammate Andretti was in the pits saying his goodbyes; the Rodriquez/Siffert Porsche 917 took over the lead. Revson moved into second. The Solar team would have been more than pleased with this result. But Sebring had more cards to play.

Just as quickly, the now-leading 917 pulled into the pits with problems, giving the lead to number 48. The actor with a broken leg, his millionaire teammate, and a Porsche nicknamed after a fish were leading the 12 Hours of Sebring, with another Ferrari 512 (this one a coupe) running second. Ferrari's crafty team manager, Mauro Forghieri, figured they now had a chance to win if they could catch the 908 but would have to pick up the pace considerably.

Mario Andretti remembers: "He came to me and said, 'When Vaccarella comes in, I want you in the car to finish the race.' If the 917 was still running,

Judging from the casual nature of this shot, it was likely taken during practice or just prior to the start of the Sebring 12-hour race. McQueen is wearing his full-faced helmet with his back to the camera, a giant "Solar Racing" logo embroidered on the back of his racing suit. Peter Revson can be seen nearer the car, putting on his helmet. *Dave Friedman*

there was no way. But when it came in with problems, a win for us looked do-able, as our Ferrari was a lot faster than the 908." Andretti hopped in at the next stop and took out after Revson. The only issue was that the Ferrari team was sure he would have to pit for fuel again before the finish. "But my job was to drive 10/10ths, no matter what. I caught Revson and passed him clean." All McQueen could do was watch from the pit wall.

True enough, Andretti's fuel light flickered just a few laps from the checkered flag. Even though he had a substantial lead, he had to go in for a splash-and-go pit stop. Just as Andretti pulled out of his pit, Revson flashed by. Andretti drew on every bit of his otherworldly talent and set out into the night after the 908. "I just went after him, not knowing if we had two or three laps to go. I caught him under

braking on that same lap and passed him again. Poor Pete. He was just spent." In one of the most breathtaking finishes in motorsport history, Andretti won by 23.8 seconds—after 12 hours of racing. Revson and McQueen finished first in the 3.0-liter category and, against all odds, a storybook second overall.

It's long been thought that Andretti took issue with McQueen's participation in the race. Not true. Mario's main concern was that if McQueen and Revson won, the Hollywood star would garner all the publicity, and his friend Peter Revson's Herculean effort would get lost in the shuffle. "McQueen was respectable," said the Indy, Daytona, and two-time Sebring winner, "especially because he drove with his leg in a cast. It must have been tough. So credit where credit is due." McQueen was given the race's Hayden Williams

Another fine photo of McQueen in the 908, this time under braking. Harry Hurst was a young track photographer at the time and has since published a photo essay entitled *12 Hours of Sebring, 1970*, which documents the entire Porsche/Ferrari battle that year. A worthy read. *Harry Hurst*

Above: Mario Andretti, Sebring, 1970. *Harry Hurst*
Right: Oblivious to the crowd of groupies just behind him, McQueen sits on the pit wall late in the race. *Harry Hurst*

Nighttime Sebring pit action. It's hard to tell who was getting in and who was getting out of the car, but Revson appears to be donning his helmet for his final stint. The previously all-white 908 now sports some subtle pinstriping on its nose. Wonder if Von Dutch dropped by to add his touch prior to the car's appearance in Florida? *Dave Friedman*

Memorial Sportsmanship Award for having competed with a broken foot and finishing so well.

While the long race with a broken foot taxed him as he prepared for the film, the making of *Le Mans* during the summer of 1970 was a debilitating personal experience for McQueen. Although he ably drove the manic Porsche 917s during filming, the emotional and challenged production of his ultimate racing movie bankrupted Solar Productions and Cinema Center Films. His marriage to Neile also hit rock bottom. The entire ordeal tainted motor racing for the actor-driver. His near-win at Sebring that year was his final, and ultimate, major ride.

If anything, McQueen's day job got in the way of his passion for motorsports. In 11 years, he'd progressed from the wheel of a sports car to a sports racer to a Formula car to an all-conquering, 240-plus mile-per-hour prototype racing machine. He demonstrated considerable skill in all of them. It's a shame he was never able to concentrate on racing—to really focus on it and apply himself in a consistent manner—due of course to his meteoric rise to fame as an actor.

What could he have achieved as a professional racing driver had he chosen to accept John Cooper's offer in 1962 to join his factory-sponsored team, and thus exit the road to stardom? We'll never know.

In this case, second was indeed good enough. The best the Solar 908 team could have reasonably hoped for was a first in class. To achieve that, and to finish second overall while challenging the 5.0-liter class machines for the win, was a huge accomplishment. A tired, but happy Peter Revson and Steve McQueen enjoyed the crowd's accolades. *Harry Hurst*

Porsche's Rico Steinemann celebrates with Steve and Neile at the postrace celebration the day after Sebring. The trophies in front of McQueen are for his second-place finish and the Hayden Williams Memorial Sportsmanship award. Wonder if that's a check in his hand? *Porsche Werkphoto*

2 Sec. D—Sun., Mar. 22, 1970 Los Angeles Times 3★

McQueen Second Behind Andretti

SEBRING, Fla. (UPI)—Mario Andretti, his leading Ferrari forced out at the 11th hour, leaped into another of the blood red cars and charged back to win the 12 Hours of Sebring Saturday night, 23.8 seconds ahead of a Porsche driven by actor Steve McQueen and cosmetics heir Peter Revson.

It was the wildest finish in the 20 runnings of this oldest of U.S. endurance races.

Pedro Rodriguez of Mexico and Jo Siffert in a factory Porsche 917 grabbed the lead an hour from the finish when the Ferrari of Andretti and Arturio Merzario of Italy, leading nearly all day, quit with a broken gearbox.

Wheel Bearing Breaks

Rodriguez, at the wheel, stretched his lead to a minute and a half over the dogged private 908 of McQueen and Revson, with Revson at the wheel. But 27 minutes from the finish, Rodriguez's car broke a wheel bearing and fell back to finish fourth.

An Alfa Romeo Spyder driven by Masten Gregory and Toine Hezmans of Holland took third.

Fifth was a Matra driven by Henri Pescarolo and Johnny Servoz-Gain of France.

Merzario was at the wheel when the lead Ferrari broke. Andretti, in the pits, was rushed into the other remaining factory 512S, driven until then by Nino Vacarella and Ignazio Giunti of Italy, running fourth at that time—about 45 minutes from the finish.

Andretti took the lead at 11:37 and widened it to about 30 seconds over Revson in the pursuing Porsche. But as he neared the end of the next-to-last lap, the main fuel tank ran out on the Ferrari.

Andretti switched to the small reserve tank and hurtled into the pits, where the usually-frantic Ferrari mechanics smoothly poured a couple of gallons of gas into the car and had him back on the track in less than 10 seconds.

"I never thought we'd be able to pull it off," said Andretti. "This was the toughest race I ever ran"—including his victory in last year's Indianapolis 500.

Andretti said his co-winners, Vacarella and Giunti, "are the ones who deserve most of the credit. I just stepped in at the last minute to give them a hand."

The Alfa in third was three minutes—more than a lap—behind the first two cars. The limping Rodriguez Porsche, which lost 10 minutes and the race with the burned wheel bearing, was four laps back.

The winning car covered 1,290 miles at an average speed of more than 113 m.p.h. The record is 115.64.

Mike Parkes of England and Chuck Parsons of Deerfield, Ill., came in sixth in a Ferrari and seventh was a Porsche 908 driven by Hans Dieter of Germany and Tony Dean of England.

McQueen competed with a cast on his left foot which was broken two weeks ago in a motorcycle race. He was allowed to drive only after agreeing to wear a special boot and fireproof socks. He glued sandpaper to the bottom of the cast to get traction on the foot that worked the clutch.

He and Revson alternated for 90-minute stretches. McQueen soaked his foot while Revson drove.

Chapter 4

McQUEEN ON TWO WHEELS

A Husqvarna 405 at about 12,000 rpm—that's music. In bike racing, I specialize; I do rough-country riding, the long-distance kind of thing. With a cycle, you're dealing with natural terrain, you learn to read the earth. . . I like being out there in the desert on a set of wheels. You're really alive out there.

—Steve McQueen, from *Star on Wheels*, 1972

It was inevitable that Steve McQueen and motorcycles

would form a lifelong link. His childhood and rough early years—scrabbling for work, living in near poverty—forced the issue on two fronts. One, bikes were cheaper than cars. Two, he was of the ideal temperament for motorcycling in the late 1940s, when the activity was far from genteel. Indeed, the personality of the rough-and-tumble biker stereotype had long been formed by then, supported by daredevil racers of the 1910s and 1920s and only given a unified visual identity we recognize today by so-called outlaws of the 1960s. In between, we had Brando and Elvis and James Dean—misunderstood, troubled, in trouble, and, for that matter, out for trouble. It would be no surprise to find a rudderless youth, enticed by the image, stick to it as a way of submerging his troubles.

William Claxton

Although a devoted Indian and Triumph fan, McQueen owned and rode many other brands, including this Honda CA77 Dream Touring. Reading a script in the studio parking lot, 1961. *Photofest*

Opposite: A happy couple, looking happy aboard a Triumph Bonneville for the July 12, 1963, issue of *Life*. The McQueens were the toast of Hollywood throughout much of the 1960s.

McQueen might be placed in this category after a cursory examination, but that would do him a tremendous injustice. Even if he didn't start out to be one of his period's most celebrated motorcycle enthusiasts, McQueen had most certainly become one. Whether you consider his positioning of motorcycles (among other fast vehicles) in his films and public life or stop to ponder the fact that, at one point, he owned more than 100 motorcycles at one time, you can't read much about McQueen and not realize that he was, deep down and to the core, a pure enthusiast, a

man for whom motorcycling was, you might say, second only to breathing. The endeavor was both an escape from acting and a validation of his skills, plus an opportunity to join a tight fraternity of riders who, at first, didn't care who he was as much as how well he could ride. These statements would, no doubt, horrify McQueen, who was as taciturn about his hobby as anyone.

The difficulty to tracing the post-McQueen history of many of his bikes is the nature of the beast. Motorcycles as a rule are more fragile, more likely

LIFE

Conservatives Take G.O.P. Lead
THE GOLDWATER RUSH

STEVE McQUEEN   Problem kid becomes a star

THE STEVE
McQUEENS
OUT RIDING

JULY 12 · 1963 · 25¢

to be dropped, broken up as parts mules for other bikes, scrapped, or simply abandoned, than cars. No doubt some of the bikes adorning his stable were not considered important in this period and were often overlooked as daily-drivers, beaters, or parts bikes. After McQueen's death in 1980, many bikes were bequeathed to friends and family, and a large selection was sold at auction in 1984 (see Chapter 5).

It would be fair to separate McQueen's motorcycles into two categories: those he loved and those he utterly adored. In his last half decade, McQueen began to collect a great variety of motorcycles, as his fame and fortune would assure, returning often to his favored brands of Indian and Triumph, but also exploring a host of other nearly forgotten brands of which remained only a handful of examples.

1946 Indian Chief

According to biographer William Nolan, it was in the fall of 1951 that McQueen had "saved enough to buy a battered cycle with a sidecar, which he proudly tooled around the Village. 'It was my first bike and I loved it,' admitted Steve. 'But I was going with a girl who began to hate the cycle—just hated riding in the bumpy sidecar. She told me, "Either the cycle goes or I go!" 'Well, there was no contest. She went.'" McQueen was working in New York and that battered cycle was a 1946 Indian Chief with a sidecar. Unfortunately, few details are available on this motorcycle and sidehack.

In that postwar (and pre–Cold War) period, Indian and Harley-Davidson big-bore models ruled the land. The Indian Chief was remarkable for its art deco–swooped fenders, a stylistic trademark that, in fact, hindered the bike's performance; those huge fenders were hefty steel stampings. But in other ways, the Chief was advanced. Where the Harleys of the time made due with rigid rear frames—the sole suspension action came from the tire itself—the Indians had rudimentary rear suspension thanks to a shock-mounted rear axle. The fork was a springer articulated-arm arrangement with a single, central shock absorber.

The flathead (or side-valve, as the valve stems were pointed down, and the combustion chamber

McQueen aboard his Triumph 650 while competing in the 1964 International Six Days Trials. Here, he pushes out from the impound area just prior to the start of the first day of competition. *Lynn Wineland*

offset over to the valve pocket) V-twin engine was mounted rigidly to the mild-steel frame; to help reduce rider fatigue and improve comfort, the large tractor-like saddle was spring-mounted to the rear frame. Also typical of the period, the '46 Chief would have had a foot clutch operated by the left foot and a hand shifter for the three-speed transmission just outboard of the left side of the teardrop fuel tank. The rider would roll off the throttle, clutch with the left foot, reach his left hand from the handlebar to the shifter, make the shift, ease in some throttle as the left foot gradually released the clutch. It's little wonder bikes with a wide torque curve—less shifting overall—were prized.

In the early 1950s, the Indian Chief was a common sight on American roads, vying with FL-series Harleys (by then already using an overhead-valve design) for sales supremacy. What was probably not clear to McQueen or any American rider of the time was that Indian was on the fast track to oblivion. A series of technical missteps and financial difficulties would see the grand old firm cease production of its own models by the end of 1953. With that, an interesting chapter in motorcycle history had closed, but, as we would later see, McQueen would remain an avid fan of the marque, with Indians a prominent part of his overall collection.

McQueen is said to have owned a K Model Harley-Davidson in New York, racing both legitimately at the drag strip and illicitly on the street. Harley's K model was a precursor to the famed Sportster, a stripped-down, 750-cc flathead V-twin that would go on to dominate dirt-track racing in the United States. In addition, McQueen took a mid-1950s BSA 650 to Cuba.

In *Steve McQueen: Star on Wheels*, McQueen said: "I had my 650 BSA and my buddies each had their rigs—a one-lung Norton Manx and a 500 BMW—and we all cycled down to Key West and took the TMT ferry across to Havana. Castro and Batista were shootin' at each other about then, and things were a little tense. I tried to sell a guy some cigarettes and got thrown in jail on a charge of pushing American contraband. I wired Neile for the money I needed to get sprung, but she was mad at me for leavin' her in New York and said no. Ended up selling my crash helmet and some parts off the BSA to bail myself out of there and get back home."

His break came in 1956 with a guest shot on *Trackdown*, which led to *Wanted: Dead or Alive*, which in turn was being filmed in Los Angeles. McQueen's permanent move to Hollywood seemed assured. He did, of course, take his motorcycle interests with him.

1959 Triumph Bonneville

Jump ahead to 1959 and McQueen's meeting with Bud Ekins. Ekins, a Triumph motorcycle dealer at the time and an accomplished off-road racer, clearly remembers his first contact with McQueen.

"There was an actor named Dick Powell," Ekins recalls in 2007. "His son was Norman. I sold Norman a new motorcycle in, I think, 1959. He took it home, and his wife said, 'Get rid of it. Take it back.' Well, Steve was working for Four Star Productions [which produced *Wanted: Dead or Alive*, and was co-founded by Dick Powell] and would come into my shop riding on the back with Norm. Well, one day Norm said that he'd sold the bike to Steve and was wondering if the warranty was still good. I said, 'Sure, no problem,' and then he [McQueen] proceeded to hang around and be a pain in the ass for the next 25 years."

That simple exchange over a 1959 Triumph Bonneville brought McQueen into what would become a lasting friendship with Bud Ekins. No question that McQueen had found the right mentor and the right motorcycle. While American bike manufacturers remained with tried-and-true designs, and the Japanese invasion of the motorcycle market was still nearly a decade from full bloom, the hot models were the British sporting bikes. The Harley Sportster, which debuted in 1957, was arguably the fastest bike in those years; it was crude and ill-handling next to the vertical-twin Triumphs.

By the mid-1950s, Triumph was a motorcycle powerhouse, with 500-cc and 650-cc twin-cylinder motorcycles performing well on racetracks and in showrooms. What's more, in 1956, Johnny Allen captured a motorcycle speed record of 214 miles per hour at the Bonneville Salt Flats using a modified T110 engine. At the time, Triumph made hot-rod versions of its 500-cc model using, among other things, twin carbs, but had not yet created a stronger version of the 650.

All that changed in 1959 with the introduction of the Bonneville, named in honor of its speed record. The T120, as it was also known, was the quintessential sporting bike. Lean, at just over 400 pounds dry weight, and quick, the Bonneville met

On the cover of *Modern Cycle* magazine, September 1965, which covered McQueen and the American team's participation in the ISDT.

with success in the United States largely on the basis of its performance. McQueen's Bonneville was a first-year model, distinctive by its headlight nacelle and valanced fenders. Triumph quickly recognized the error, and for 1960 produced a revised Bonneville with TR6-like thin chrome fenders and a stood-proud chrome headlight.

The destiny of McQueen's particular bike is unknown. It is believed to have been sold off or given away early in McQueen's career, amid the typically high turnover rate of the breed. Moreover, McQueen had caught another kind of bug, one that struck his fancy almost by accident. Supposedly, he'd been riding with actor friend Dennis Hopper—considered perhaps ironic today, as McQueen often commented that the biker movies of the 1960s had "set motorcycling back 200 years"—and noticed dirt riders on some open cliffs in west Los Angeles.

McQueen said, "I first tried out dirt riding on a bike I'd borrowed from a neighbor, and the sense of being out there on your own was tremendous. No preparation. Just kick it over, drive up the side of a hill—and you're free!" That freedom was something important to McQueen and had piqued his interest in dirt riding. He began to ask questions of Ekins at his San Fernando Valley shop. "He saw all those Triumphs at the back with no headlights and was curious about those, too," Ekins recalls in 2007. "I agreed to take him out and show him the ropes."

Soon, McQueen was racing off-road in Southern California, mainly on TR6 Triumphs prepped for racing with higher, braced handlebars and knobby tires. At that time, the differences between full-on street bikes and dirt racers were minimal, and it would be several years before purpose-built dirt race bikes would become common. Only a few years after that, the category further specialized, with bikes designed just for high-speed desert racing, picking along slow but difficult trails (enduro), closed-course dirt racing (motocross), an ultra-low-speed, obstacle-bashing ballet called trials, and, finally, crossover vehicles that could be used on the street as well as in the woods.

But McQueen's early dirt-riding experience came astride the Triumph. After riding in a series of West Coast events and doing well under Ekins' tutelage, McQueen took a role in *The Great Escape*, directed by John Sturges. It would be a seminal role for McQueen, not just for his acting ability, but in forging his reputation for putting fast cars and motorcycles into his films.

As discussed in the last chapter, McQueen and Ekins stuck with modified Triumphs for the filming of *The Great Escape*. With their rigid frames, the WWII-era BMWs the Triumphs portrayed weren't tough enough or fast enough for the stunts they had in mind. And despite the impression from watching the camouflaged Triumphs on screen that they'd been thoroughly rigged for the job, that's not the case. "We had stock bikes. Standard shocks, but a lighter front wheel," recalls Ekins. The TR6s—two were used, purchased by MGM from Ekins' own store—were often taken out by McQueen after daily shooting for joyriding.

Smile, boys! America's Triumph-riding 1964 ISDT team, from left: Dave Ekins, Bud Ekins, McQueen, and Cliff Coleman. McQueen did not compete wearing the cast; it was removed prior to the start of the event. *Lynn Wineland*

After shooting, the actual bikes used in the film are believed to have been sold in Europe, although it's likely one of them made it back to the States; no matter, their whereabouts are unknown. However, for a recent exhibit at the Petersen Automotive Museum in Los Angeles, Triumph collector Sean Kelly created a tribute bike, starting with a '62 TR6. The headlight wears the required dimming slit, and the knee pads are classic BMW-style designs. The solo saddle and simple luggage rack look just like those fitted to the real TR6s in the film.

Returning from Europe, and after wrapping *Love with the Proper Stranger* in New York, McQueen resumed his desert racing, including the 1963 running of the Greenhorn Enduro in and around Mojave. His Triumph lost a cylinder halfway through, but he finished the race. By that time, McQueen's insatiable appetite for two-wheeled speed had him at the track or in the desert whenever his shooting schedule allowed, but he continued to race in the Novice class. He didn't race enough to earn sufficient points to run with the Experts. But that didn't mean he was left out of international competition; in fact, the Greenhorn would be his training ground for the International Six Days Trials (ISDT).

1964 Triumph TR6SC ISDT

In 1964, Bud Ekins put together the first American team to contest the ISDT, held that year in East Germany. It consisted of Bud, brother Dave Ekins, McQueen, Cliff Coleman, and John Steen. Bud the Triumph dealer and longtime stalwart of the brand elected to run in the 500-cc class with T100SCs for himself, Dave, and Steen, while a pair of TR6SCs were destined for Coleman and McQueen to run in the 750-cc class.

The ISDT that year was grueling, with constant rain, unfamiliar terrain, and world-class competition. McQueen was at a disadvantage right from the start, as he'd raced and practiced in the arid California desert. And yet they were immediately competitive, ending the second day tied in points for the lead with Britain. McQueen told Nolan, "At this stage, I was definitely lined up for a gold medal and going hard. Part of the last run of this second day was over an open road cutting through a forest. I was dicing with the British champ, Jon Gills, a marvelous racer, and we were moving along at full chat in the rain. We could figure where the highway would bend by watching the way the trees lined up. But we got fooled because at one point the trees marched straight ahead while the road turned. We came into this turn, full turkey leg, at about eighty—and began sliding for traction. I went off the road and down into a cart truck, taking a fall. I saw marks where other riders had got themselves into the same kind of trouble. My cheek was cut from the goggles but nothing was broken, so I picked the twigs and leaves out of my ears and looked around for my bike. The tail pipe was smashed. I groaned, flipped a tool out of my back pocket, and bent the pipe back into usable shape."

McQueen got back on course and began to make up time. But on day three, the American team's hopes vanished as Bud Ekins broke his leg after hitting a bridge abutment, and McQueen had a run-in with a spectator on a bike, who cut across the course. "I'd survived. But my bike didn't," he later told Nolan. "I took off the front fender. The wheel was badly dented, and the tire was shot. Which might have been all right, but the forks were bent clear back to the chassis. I managed to ride back to our van, but my run was over. That spill had cost me more than a medal, it cost me the bloody race."

Bud Ekins prepared the ISDT Triumphs, although motorcycle expert Marc Cook notes that they are "just a few hour's work beyond a stock street bike." Here, McQueen gives the oil lines a final wrenching. Note extended front forks and waterproofing measures. *Lynn Wineland*

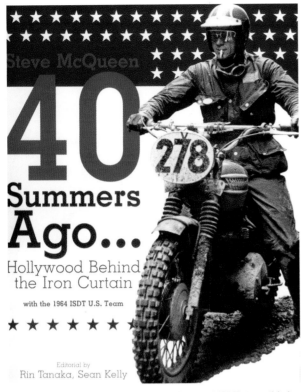

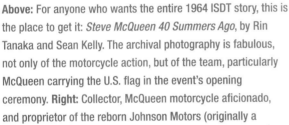

Above: For anyone who wants the entire 1964 ISDT story, this is the place to get it: *Steve McQueen 40 Summers Ago*, by Rin Tanaka and Sean Kelly. The archival photography is fabulous, not only of the motorcycle action, but of the team, particularly McQueen carrying the U.S. flag in the event's opening ceremony. **Right:** Collector, McQueen motorcycle aficionado, and proprietor of the reborn Johnson Motors (originally a Triumph dealer), Sean Kelly found the actual Triumph TR6 ridden by McQueen in the ISDT races. His race number, 278, was decided by the starting order for the trials. From the McQueen exhibit at the Petersen Automotive Museum. *Matt Stone*

McQueen's TR6SC was prepared for the 1965 ISDT, which McQueen was unable to attend. His bike was ridden by Ed Kretz Jr.

Normally, old race bikes like this are lost to time, and in fact the other four bikes from that 1964 race remain undiscovered. But after considerable research, restorer Sean Kelly tracked down McQueen's bike, VIN TR6SC-DU13287. As he writes in *Steve McQueen 40 Summers Ago. . . Hollywood Behind the Iron Curtain*, by Kelly and Rin Tanaka, McQueen's Triumph came home to Johnson Motors after the 1965 ISDT and was ridden by Bud Ekins in several major desert races in the mid-1960s. After sifting through old pink slips still in Ekins' possession, Kelly, using his knowledge of Triumph build numbers, discovered that five motorcycles registered as 1966 models were in fact built in 1964. Eventually, Kelly had the VINs of all five bikes and commenced a search for McQueen's. After what he describes as an illegal DMV search, he found the then-current owner, Frank Danielson. Danielson had fitted a sidecar to the TR6SC and won his class in the Baja 1000 three times with it.

The '64 TR6 was a significant motorcycle for Triumph on a lot of levels. It used the new unit-

continued on page 154

Celebrity has its uses as McQueen takes a ride, circa 1966, during filming of *The Sand Pebbles*, on a Suzuki road racer. Although clothed in full race-prep bodywork, the Suzuki does not appear to be any of the company's racing motorcycles for the series but probably a cafe racer version of the 250-cc X-6. *Bettmann/CORBIS*
Below left: Although he was known to be proficient mechanically, Bud Ekins says McQueen didn't do a lot of his own wrenching. This publicity shot has McQueen fiddling with his Rickman-Metisse-framed Triumph scrambler. This lightweight dirt bike used a custom frame and a modified-for-durability Triumph twin. *Kurt Gunther/MPTV.net* **Below:** Aboard his Triumph scrambler, McQueen defined the tough look. While his apparel for street riding was amazingly casual, he took his dirt racing seriously. Moreover, as can be seen here, he was a fitness nut in the 1960s, often building his own gym on the set. *Courtesy Michael Keyser*

Deerskin gloves, Persol sunglasses, Triumph scrambler: It all looked like quintessential, casual McQueen, although even a Sunday ride with him turned more often than not into a mini-GP. *Photofest*

Riding the river trail on his then-new Honda CR250 Elsinore, McQueen showed his willingness to adapt to new dirt bike technology, even if longtime friend and mentor Bud Ekins disregarded the Japanese brands. The Honda was named for the wild off-road spectacle—500 riders contested a 10-mile-long course that was a little bit of everything—that was the Elsinore Grand Prix. *Chad McQueen collection*

McQueen astride a Norton on set during the filming of *Le Mans*. He also had a Triumph and a Husqvarna with him while in France, both for pleasure riding and to get around the massive *Le Mans* course and countryside. Messenger cap and iconic Heuer Monaco watch add to that 1970s look. *Chad McQueen collection*

continued from page 151

construction 650-cc engine, which was structurally more sound and used new cylinder heads that boosted power. Those heads had additional finning for improved cooling and ran an 8.5:1 compression ratio for the Bonneville and TR6 models; the detuned Thunderbird used a 7.5:1 ratio.

Through the 1960s and even into the early 1970s, the Triumph 500-cc and 650-cc twins were the motorcycles to have, dominating in all forms of racing and showing remarkable versatility; indeed, the Triumphs of this period were capable of a broad range of successes never to be matched.

1971 Husqvarna 400CR

McQueen's dirt activities were legendary, and his competitiveness was, if such a thing is possible, growing. So it was probably no surprise when he abandoned his large, heavy, four-stroke Triumph dirt bikes for the new modern equivalent, the Husqvarna 400CR.

The Swedish manufacturer began making motorcycles in 1903 after building bicycles. But two things put Husky on the map: One, near dominance

McQueen at the Elsinore Grand Prix aboard his Husqvarna 400 Cross. The two-stroke Husky had recently appeared on the scene, sporting a massive amount of power and superb stability. McQueen also raced the Elsinore in the 250-cc class. Thanks to these fast and sturdy Swedish bikes, the days of the four-stroke desert racer were numbered.
Chester Maydole/MPTV.net

of the European motocross championships; it won 13 titles between 1959 and 1979, 10 of them before McQueen got involved. And two, the Huskys ridden by McQueen and legendary dirt racer Malcolm Smith in the movie *On Any Sunday* helped solidify the brand's place in off-road history.

McQueen's choice was the 400, which he often referred to as a "405." Its air-cooled, single-cylinder engine produced explosive power, enough to make the Husky dramatically faster than the now-outdated Triumphs. And this was despite the fact that his was an older four-speed model. The simple fact was that the 400 Husky was so powerful—the big two-stroke had prodigious torque in addition to a

As a collector, McQueen relished motorcycle swap meets, where he might find complete bikes to buy or massive lots of parts. Here he is with Charles "Red" Wolverton. McQueen paid for Wolverton to go to California to ride one of the few running Aces after discovering that he owned a bike Red had taken to victory.
Barbara Minty McQueen

dramatic top-end hit—that it might well have gotten by with one or two speeds.

The key to the Husky's prowess in the desert—in McQueen's 405-cc form and as a 125-cc and 250-cc—was low weight. Although in the following years, the Japanese manufacturers would catch Husky on power and weight, the Swedish bikes were renowned for being fast, stable, durable, and easy to work on. The company was inherently conservative and failed to take on pet technical theories until they were well proven. Moreover, Huskys were very well built with high levels of fit and finish. The marque's

instantly identifiable two-tone aluminum fuel tanks were partly painted and partly polished.

During the time McQueen owned this Husky, he offered glimpses into the freedom of off-road riding to journalists. He told Nolan: "If I see a rabbit tear off, I can chase after him. If I see some Indian petroglyphs on the rocks, I can stop there and study them . . . I just sit out there, alone, maybe for an hour or so, looking, feeling . . . with a 360-degree view of the world. Nobody to bother me." McQueen also owned another interesting Husqvarna, this one custom built with a titanium frame. This metal is

In the desert, ever-present cigarette in the pursed lips, McQueen rides his well-worn Triumph. He often said that desert racing was his "thing" for the purity of it. It gave him a sense of freedom and an identity different from that of a well-known actor. Plus, he was damn good at it. *William Claxton*

Circa 1979, McQueen on one of his beloved Indians, this one a 1941 Indian Chief. His first bike was a Chief, and he was drawn to the brand throughout his life. This one was likely restored by good friend and Indian guru Sammy Pierce. *Barbara Minty McQueen*

very strong, if a bit brittle, which was demonstrated when McQueen was out riding. He landed a hard jump, and the left side of the handlebars broke, right at the crown. So much for the exotic-framed Husky.

And, on another occasion, when talking about his home in Palm Springs: "I can drop right down into that wash and run for forty miles, all out, and maybe follow a plume of dust to find out who's behind it. Turns out to be another guy ridin' his bike same as I'm ridin' mine. We sit and rap for awhile, like in the old barnstorming days when two strangers could land their crates in a Kansas field and talk about flying."

A need to ride second only to breathing? Barely.

Left: 1921 Indian Dirt Track Racer. After World War I, Indian and Harley-Davidson fought vigorously on the racetrack. This stripped-down racer was used on the board tracks popular at the time, typically one mile in length and steeply banked. These brakeless motorcycles would average more than 100 miles per hour. *Barbara Minty McQueen* Right: McQueen's World War I–era Harley-Davidson was among the one-third of all H-Ds produced in 1917 to go the military. The suspensionless chassis was not far from its bicycle roots during this period, with a single rear brake and a hoop-style frame that encircled the engine. This bike was sold at the 1984 estate sale and now belongs to Dale Walksler. *Wheels Through Time Museum*

McQueen, the Collector

McQueen was in huge demand by the early 1970s and had disposable income to spare. With this wealth, McQueen traveled, purchased houses, and inexorably was drawn to collecting motorcycles. His partner in this pursuit, as ever, was Bud Ekins, who assisted McQueen with purchases and helped store a good many of his new finds. McQueen is believed to have had 120-plus motorcycles at any one time. He was somewhat notorious among his neighbors on the private drive in Trancas Beach, near Malibu, for clogging the streets with his many cars and bikes.

By the late 1970s, McQueen and Barbara had relocated to Santa Paula, California. He went for the airport, a narrow slash of asphalt in the valley cut by the Santa Suzanna River, because he knew he could find a home for his newly purchased Boeing Stearman biplane. But the move had other benefits, including a large hangar in which he could store a great deal of his collection, not to mention the 15 or so acres of property that came with his Santa Paula ranch house.

Chronicled below and in Chapter 5 is a small sampling of the motorcycles McQueen is known to have owned. More are suspected to have been lost in the shuffle of deals, trades, and gifts. And, for that matter, says Ekins, "You have to be careful of any bike that's supposed to have been one of Steve's. There are a lot out there that he never owned. Same for me. I once had warehouse space that I shared with a couple of guys; we put our bikes there for storage. I had a bunch of my old [Triumph dealer] letterhead around. A few years later, I hear from a guy who says, 'I have a BSA Gold Star you sold.' And I tell him, that's interesting. I've never owned a Gold Star."

The bulk of McQueen's collection in the mid-to-late 1970s was older, historically significant motorcycles. He did collect a higher percentage of Indians than other makes and was often seen riding his 1940s-vintage Indian Chief with sidecar on Pacific Coast Highway. Indeed, the newest motorcycle on the 1984 auction block was a 1974 Yamaha 360 enduro bike. That list would include a 1922 Ace (listed as "factory original, runs"), a 1970 Velocette 500, a 1913 Excelsior, a circa-1930 Matchless, and a 1912

Harley-Davidson. Most of the bikes sold at the 1984 auction went into private collections. Several were auctioned by Bonhams in late 2006. Others trade hands privately all the time, the advertisements for them nearly always beginning with "formerly owned by Steve McQueen." All in all, there were more than 200 motorcycles—enough to fill anyone's lifetime as a motorcycle enthusiast.

The Last Word

No motorcycle enthusiast can look at McQueen's two-wheeled exploits and not feel a kinship. Throughout his riding career, McQueen did it the hard way, earning the respect of the other desert competitors by racing tough, and garnering the admiration of fellow collectors by looking hard and doing his research. Barbara said that "Steve had an encyclopedic knowledge of all the motorcycles ever made and every manufacturer who had ever put them on the market." His collection, like Jay Leno's,

was created by the alchemy of a committed motorcycle nut, substantial resources, and the free time to put them into practice. With the help of longtime friend Ekins, McQueen traveled extensively to view collections as well as single motorcycles for sale. For many years, he maintained a "motorcycles wanted" ad in *Hemmings Motor News*. Asked if McQueen would leverage his fame to close the sale of a bike he particularly wanted, Ekins says, "Damn right he would. And he would get it."

In the end, McQueen purchased the bikes he wanted to own without regard for popularity or future values; he was neither showoff nor speculator. As with his racing and his acting, he lived in the moment and for the moment, merely doing what any true-to-the-core motorcycle nut would do with the same money and time. It's for this reason, layered atop his undeniable charm, considerable talent as a rider, and gritty resolve to race (and finish), that motorcyclists the world over have come to admire and deeply respect Steve McQueen.

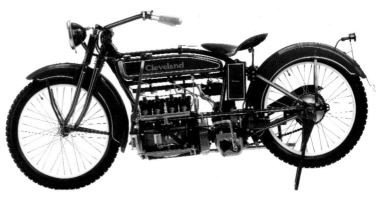

Left: Pope Manufacturing built motorcycles from 1911 to 1918. McQueen purchased this example in 1979 for a then-substantial $5,000. The 1,000-cc V-twin had many advanced features for the period, including a chain final drive, three-speed transmission, and suspension front and rear. It also had cam-operated valves for both intake and exhaust; many bikes of the period retained atmospheric intake valves. *Wheels Through Time Museum* **Right:** This 1926 Cleveland Fowler four used an inline four-cylinder engine, not unlike many automotive powerplants, although air-cooled. According to Gooding & Company, which auctioned this motorcycle from the Otis Chandler estate collection in 2006, McQueen bought the rare bike in California in 1977 and bequeathed it to Bud Ekins upon his passing. Ekins kept the Cleveland until the mid-1980s, selling it to Richard Morris. Chandler acquired it from him in 1993. It is fully restored and thought to be the only example remaining. *Gooding & Company*

McQUEEN
AS CYCLE TESTER

cQueen opens a feature appearing in the November 1966 issue of *Popular Science* with these words: "First of all, I don't set myself up as an expert on either setting up machinery for racing, or the actual sport of racing itself. But after 2½ years of desert riding in Southern California, TT Scrambles, Hare and Hound, and a bit of racing in the wet in the Six Day Trials in East Germany in 1964, I sure hope I picked up a little about motorcycles and riding along the way." Whether inserted by an editor or offered by McQueen himself, this admission is central to his attitude toward racing. Never feeling as though his celebrity should buy access, McQueen was driven to compete on level terms, to be rewarded for performance not just an appearance.

McQueen was also quick to thank his longtime friends and riding partners, Bud and Dave Ekins. Being "partners" in a cycle shop in the San Fernando Valley had "been a keen education—like going to school. . . . they are two of the best desert bike riders this country has ever produced."

McQueen prefaced his comments on the bikes stating, "Here are my impressions of the bikes and how I rate them for desert riding—the kind of riding I'm mainly interested in."

"The BSA Hornet.
The first bike I tested—the BSA Hornet—is designed for desert riding or scrambles. . . . It's a keen bike. But I found it awfully heavy. A lot of weight would have to be stripped off to make the bike competitive. . . . The Hornet also had a tendency to want to go its own way. I always had to stay on top of it. I also think the front forks should be raked on a more forward angle. With this adjustment, the BSA would have a more stable ride in the rough and would be generally a smoother performer.

"The Norton-Matisse.
This is a TT bike with trials tires and no knobby treads. It's a 750-cc

four-stroke, two-cylinder that has lots of torque. It's a handful. This semi-custom model isn't a true scrambler. It's more of a TT, or track racing bike, because of its shorter forks, which give you less ground clearance than I like a scrambler to have. Norton's history in road racing is well known, but desert riding is a bit different.

"The Triumph Bonneville.
My feeling has been that the Triumph Bonneville 650-cc has been best for the desert until recently, when the lightweight started to nip at its tail. It has more wins in desert racing than any other bike. It, too, is of the brute variety. The geometry of the Bonneville's suspension is set up for oversteer, and it handles real good. Its weight is competitive. The electrical system can be somewhat unreliable, but once sorted out it usually stays sorted out.

"The Honda.
They have learned a great deal at Honda about desert riding. And they have set up the Honda Scrambler accordingly—good electrical system, super suspension, and a very good powertrain. They can be made to perform like a 500-cc and you have a lot of rpm to play with. It's a keen bike for the money.

"The Greeves and Montessa.
Despite my preference for four-strokes, I was surprised at the performance of these two-stroke bikes. The Montessa is a Spanish import with a 250-cc engine. It's a great bike—a keen bike—and a comer. The Greeves Challenger is also a high-revving two-stroke that has been very successful in European scrambles. It's strictly a race-bred vehicle. A very healthy piece of machinery, it has even more beans than the Montessa. The two-strokes have a lot going for them, but frankly I'm too attached to the four-strokes to be completely won over.

"A hybrid bike.
I prefer the big four-stroke engine but on a light bike. The best way I've found to

Actor-turned-guest-tester McQueen commented on a group of dirt bikes for *Popular Science*, a gambit to get Steve to ride a bunch of cool bikes and, no doubt, to sell a few magazines with his likeness on the cover. It worked for all parties concerned.

get this combination is with a bike I put together with the assistance of the Ekins brothers in our valley shop. I used a Rickman-Matisse frame—a revolutionary piece of equipment that does away with the oil tanks. I used the 650-cc Triumph engine as a powerplant for this bike. It has Ceriani forks with 7½ inches of travel for a real smooth ride, and a BSA crown. The rig is the best handling bike I've ever owned. And the power—it's supersonic.

"Summing up, I'd say they're a high-performing group of bikes and I had a ball riding them." Even if he was being kind to some of the bikes he didn't fall in love with, the last part of that statement was surely the whole, unvarnished truth.

Chapter 5

AN ENDURING LEGACY

I'm an all-American rebel, Making my big getaway
Yeah, you know it's time, I gotta fly
Like Steve McQueen, All I need's a fast machine
I'm gonna make it all right
Like Steve McQueen, Underneath your radar screen
You'll never catch me tonight

From Sheryl Crow's hit single, *Steve McQueen*, 2002

Steve McQueen passed away in Mexico on November 7,

1980. He died from complications of mesothelioma, a rare and painful form of lung cancer that few survive. The events surrounding the discovery that he had cancer, treatment attempts, and his final surrender have been recounted in numerous books, so there's no need to detail them here. Suffice it to say that even though he hoped to beat the odds, he knew there was a chance that he would not and put certain of his affairs in order. Among them was the disposition of his impressive stable of cars, trucks, motorcycles, and airplanes.

Some were given away to friends, a few "sold for a dollar," so as to call it a purchase instead of a gift. Others were specifically willed, such his two most significant Porsches. "For some reason, Dad wanted me to have the '58 Speedster," recalls Chad, "I don't really know why; it was the last thing I cared about at the time. Perhaps it was because that's the first car Dad went racing in. He'd sold it once before, bought it back, and didn't want to see it ever leave the family again." The 1969 Porsche 911S, which McQueen had owned since new, went to his daughter, Terry. When she passed away in March 1998 due to respiratory failure, this 911 also became

Chad McQueen collection

Chad's. Two of Steve McQueen's fabulous Porsches were together again in the same garage, reunited, sadly, by a pair of unhappy circumstances, nearly 18 years apart. Chad also inherited several of his father's most prized motorcycles.

It took several years to settle the many aspects of McQueen's estate, but the family held an auction in 1984. Managed by the Kruse auction company, the Steve McQueen Estate Auction was held at the Imperial Palace hotel (well known for its own large and significant automobile collection) in Las Vegas on November 24 and 25.

It was an event that car people and McQueen faithfuls still talk about. Seventeen cars, including his favorite XK-SS, the Allard, three Packards, several trucks, the '49 Cadillc, both of his comfy old Hudsons, the Von Dutch–built Winton replica from *The Reivers*, and the '51 Chevy convertible he drove so hamfistedly in *The Hunter* went on the block. Significant as it was, the automobile offerings pale somewhat in comparison to the assemblage of motorcycles and parts. Approximately 95 motorcycles, plus another dozen that were classified as parts bikes or merely pallets of bits and pieces, crossed the block. Indians, Harleys, dirt racers, Triumphs. The prices obtained matter little. Steve McQueen's four- and two-wheeled toys ended up in the hands of people who wanted them and who loved him.

Ford Motor Company has had a big hand in furthering McQueen's legacy. The first salvo was a TV commercial for the Ford Puma. Even though this new model was not destined for sale in the United States, Ford elected to create a tie-in with *Bullitt*. Although the '68 Mustang used in the film and the subcompact, front-wheel-drive Puma sport coupe don't have much in common, the real message is Steve McQueen's drawing power as an international star.

The commercial was shot in San Francisco just prior to the car's 1997 launch and a bit less than 30 years after *Bullitt* was filmed there. Computer-generated animation (CGA) was not as widespread or sophisticated in the mid-1990s as it is today. This commercial is not only a brilliant stroke from a creative standpoint, but the CGA is beautifully done and a bit startling the first time you see it. It shows a digitally recreated Steve McQueen, in full *Bullitt*

Each lot from the estate auction came with a certificate of authenticity signed by Chad and Terry. When it comes to collectible cars and bikes, provenance is everything. Providing this sort of documentation was a wise move on behalf of the estate and the auction company, as it will only grow in significance as time goes on.

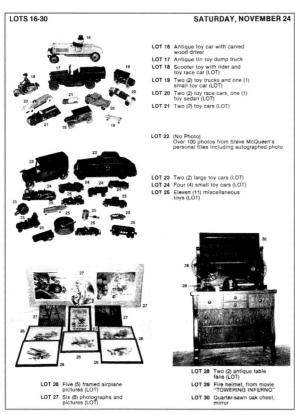

LOT 16 Antique toy car with carved wood driver

LOT 17 Antique tin toy dump truck

LOT 18 Scooter toy with rider and toy race car (LOT)

LOT 19 Two (2) toy trucks and one (1) small toy car (LOT)

LOT 20 Two (2) toy race cars, one (1) toy sedan (LOT)

LOT 21 Two (2) toy cars (LOT)

LOT 22 (No Photo) Over 100 photos from Steve McQueen's personal files including autographed photo

LOT 23 Two (2) large toy cars (LOT)

LOT 24 Four (4) small toy cars (LOT)

LOT 25 Eleven (11) miscellaneous toys (LOT)

LOT 26 Five (5) framed airplane pictures (LOT)

LOT 27 Six (6) photographs and pictures (LOT)

LOT 28 Two (2) antique table fans (LOT)

LOT 29 Fire helmet, from movie "TOWERING INFERNO"

LOT 30 Quarter-sawn oak chest, mirror

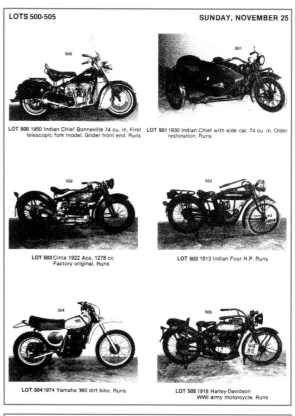

LOT 500 1950 Indian Chief Bonneville 74 cu. in. First telescopic fork model. Glider front end. Runs

LOT 501 1930 Indian Chief with side car. 74 cu. in. Older restoration. Runs

LOT 502 Circa 1922 Ace. 1278 cc Factory original. Runs

LOT 503 1913 Indian Four H.P. Runs

LOT 504 1974 Yamaha 360 dirt bike. Runs

LOT 505 1918 Harley-Davidson WWI army motorcycle. Runs

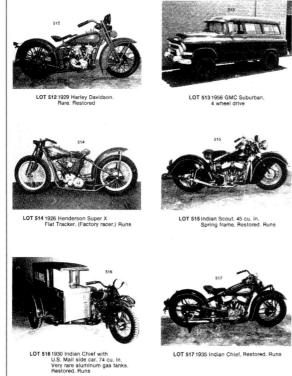

LOT 512 1929 Harley Davidson. Rare. Restored

LOT 513 1956 GMC Suburban. 4 wheel drive

LOT 514 1926 Henderson Super X Flat Tracker. (Factory racer.) Runs

LOT 515 Indian Scout. 45 cu. in. Spring frame. Restored. Runs

LOT 516 1930 Indian Chief with U.S. Mail side car. 74 cu. in. Very rare aluminum gas tanks. Restored. Runs

LOT 517 1935 Indian Chief. Restored. Runs

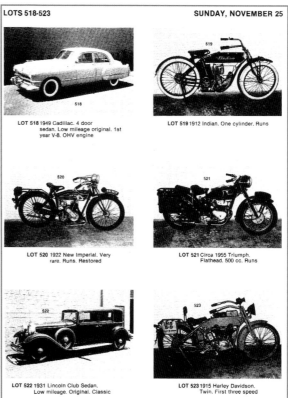

LOT 518 1949 Cadillac. 4 door sedan. Low mileage original. 1st year V-8. OHV engine

LOT 519 1912 Indian. One cylinder. Runs

LOT 520 1922 New Imperial. Very rare. Runs. Restored

LOT 521 Circa 1955 Triumph. Flathead. 500 cc. Runs

LOT 522 1931 Lincoln Club Sedan. Low mileage. Original. Classic

LOT 523 1915 Harley Davidson. Twin. First three speed

Each catalog for the 1984 Estate Auction in Las Vegas was numbered. The event was held just after the fourth anniversary of his passing.

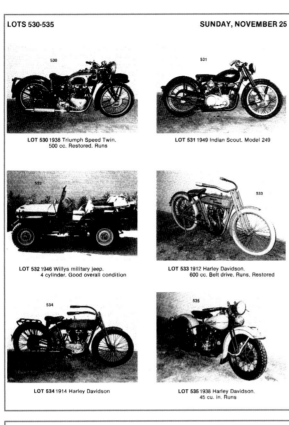

LOT 530 1938 Triumph Speed Twin.
500 cc. Restored. Runs

LOT 531 1949 Indian Scout. Model 249

LOT 532 1946 Willys military jeep.
4 cylinder. Good overall condition

LOT 533 1912 Harley Davidson.
600 cc. Belt drive. Runs. Restored

LOT 534 1914 Harley Davidson

LOT 535 1938 Harley Davidson.
45 cu. in. Runs

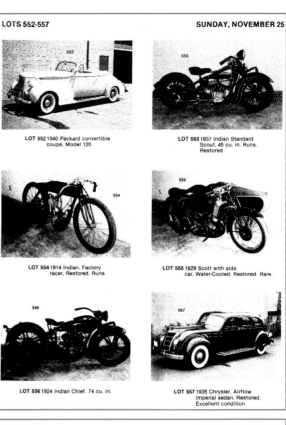

LOT 552 1940 Packard convertible
coupe. Model 120

LOT 553 1937 Indian Standard
Scout. 45 cu. in. Runs.
Restored

LOT 554 1914 Indian. Factory
racer. Restored. Runs

LOT 555 1929 Scott with side
car. Water-Cooled. Restored. Rare.

LOT 556 1924 Indian Chief. 74 cu. in.

LOT 557 1935 Chrysler. Airflow
Imperial sedan. Restored.
Excellent condition.

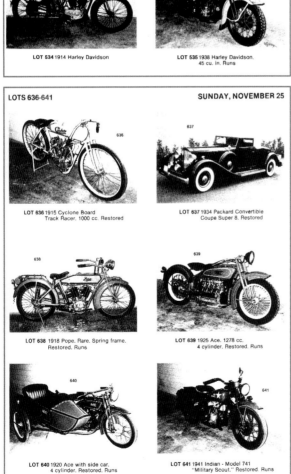

LOT 636 1915 Cyclone Board
Track Racer. 1000 cc. Restored

LOT 637 1934 Packard Convertible
Coupe Super 8. Restored

LOT 638 1918 Pope. Rare. Spring frame.
Restored. Runs

LOT 639 1925 Ace. 1278 cc.
4 cylinder. Restored. Runs

LOT 640 1920 Ace with side car.
4 cylinder. Restored. Runs

LOT 641 1941 Indian - Model 741
"Military Scout." Restored. Runs

LOT 655 1953 Allard Roadster.
Chrysler powered.

LOT 656 1942 Indian Chief.
Military model. 74 cu. in.
Restored. Runs

LOT 657 1914 Pope Model K. Rare. Belt drive.
Restored. Runs

LOT 658 1932 Harley Davidson VL
with side car. 74 cu. in.

LOT 659 1914 Yale. Restored

LOT 660 1927 Indian Chief. 74 cu. in.
Restored. Runs

Steve McQueen, digitally reborn for the making of two Ford commercials. Note the right-hand-drive seating position in the Puma. A good bit of computer work must have been required to put him not only in a car much smaller than the '68 Mustang but move the image to the right front seating position as well. *Ford*

garb, driving the new car throughout the city. The *Bullitt* soundtrack plays in the background. Some of the shots show McQueen at the wheel of the Mustang, and they are quick cuts so you can't really tell what he's driving. Others, however, put him clearly inside the Puma, and the effect is as seamless as could be expected.

The final scene shows McQueen backing the Puma into a carport, also occupied by Dave Kunz's '68 Mustang GT (see Chapter 2) and a motorcycle. McQueen contemplates the bike and his old steed, then pats the fender of the Puma. If there's anything to take issue with, it's the appearance of a chrome "horse and corral" in the grille of Kunz's Mustang. In *Bullitt*, the original car's grille is devoid of the badging and fog lights a '68 GT would have. But, according to Kunz, one of the storyboards for the commercial showed the familiar horse emblem, and the director wasn't about to argue with what the creative team called for. So a search went out, and a local used parts vendor had the piece. The director offered him several times market value for it, as long as he could deliver it to the set immediately. He did, and it was installed on Kunz's car for the shot. When filming was done, Kunz promptly removed the incorrect piece and gave it to one of the crewmembers that had a Mustang. You can see the Puma commercial video on numerous video websites or at www.mcqueenonline.com.

Ford's vice president of global design, J Mays, is a McQueen fan and is well known for mining a company's history as a source of inspiration for future models. He and staff design manager Doug Gaffka felt the updated-for-1999 Ford Mustang was ripe for the *Bullitt* treatment and developed a concept car that was revealed at the Los Angeles Auto Show in 2000. Painted Highland Green with a black leather interior and riding on alloy updates of the original American Racing Torq-Thrust D, the Bullitt Mustang Concept was a hit with the media and public alike. It didn't take much convincing to get the project greenlighted for limited production, which was announced a year later, also at the L.A. show.

The Bullitt Mustang was offered only in 2001 and only in the coupe body style. The modifications were straightforward but highly effective. Most were painted Highland Green, but not wanting to limit its appeal, Ford chose to offer the car in black or a dark metallic blue as well. The standard GT's 4.6-liter V-8 received a larger throttle body intake, high-flow mufflers, and underdrive alternator and water pump pulleys. The result was a modest 5 horsepower increase (from 260 to 265), although the sound that pours out of the special brushed stainless-steel exhaust pipes is special. Like the movie car, all '01 Bullitt Mustangs are equipped with manual transmission.

continued on page 170

The first track on Sheryl Crow's *c'mon, c'mon* CD is entitled *Steve McQueen*. Dave Kunz's '68 Bullitt tribute Mustang was used in the making of the song's video. And Sheryl Crow, indeed, was there, as evidenced by her autograph on the doorjamb. *Evan Klein*

Chad participated in the press launch program in San Francisco for the Bullitt-edition Mustang. He's seen here with the new car and Dave Kunz's '68. He also took the opportunity to give the press car a brief flight (opposite), in honor of the stunt work his dad, Bud Ekins, and Carey Loftin performed there 33 years earlier. *Ford*

The badge on the rear fascia is all you need to know about this 2001 limited-edition Ford Mustang. *Ford*

The beat goes on: Ford snuck us this stylised illustration of the 2008 Bullitt-edition Mustang, looking shadowy in Highland Green, of course. Another instant collectible is born. *Ford Design*

TAG Heuer celebrates the legend of *Le Mans* with a reissued line of Monaco watches. McQueen's likeness was also used in several advertisements. The watch with the black face (below) is the latest special-edition Monaco, with blue and orange stripes and a Gulf Oil logo in honor of the Gulf-Wyer-liveried 917s used in the film. The blue-faced piece (top) with the black leather strap is an original 1969 Heuer Monaco, just like the one McQueen wore in the movie. *TAG Heuer*

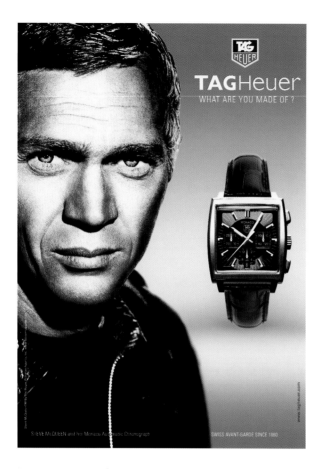

continued from page 167

Exterior revisions include unique side scoops, 17-inch five-spoke alloy wheels patterned after the above-noted American Torq-Thursts, and a brushed-aluminum fuel filler door. Like the original, the nouveau Bullitt Mustang is largely devoid of chrome trim. The car's ride height was lowered about 3/4 inch, and the suspension was fitted with Tokico gas shocks and revised front and rear antiroll bars. Thirteen-inch Brembo front brake rotors were also added. Inside, the Bullitt featured charcoal leather sport seats, a brushed-aluminum shifter ball, shifter bezel, door sill plates with Bullitt badging, and aluminum pedal covers. The graphics on the instrument gauges were redone to resemble a 1960s style. Ford built 5,582 '01 Bullitt Mustangs, and they were considered collectible the minute they were put on sale. The first four cars were specially numbered, with the Bullitt Mustang 01 and 02 going to the McQueen family.

Besides the amazing, now-priceless array of cars that appeared in *Le Mans*, another accoutrement that often catches the eye is the unique Heuer Monaco wristwatch worn by the Michael Delaney character throughout the film. This avant-garde, square-cased design was launched in 1969, just prior to the commencement of filming. The company (now TAG Heuer) elected to reintroduce the Monaco model in 1998 as one of several heritage-inspired, car-related watch lines.

Although the piece McQueen wore in the movie is a stainless-steel, two-dial chronograph with a blue face and a black leather strap, the reintroduced Monaco is offered not only in this look (model CW2113) but in many varieties: two- and three-dial chronographs and nonchronograph movements, stainless-steel or gold case, metal bracelet or leather band, and so forth. The proportions between old and new vary somewhat, and the winding stem has been relocated from the left to the right side of the case.

Several of McQueen's street and race cars have been commissioned as die-cast models. These include his XK-SS, the '68 Mustang fastback from *Bullitt*, and the Solar Productions Porsche 917. All of these examples are 1/18th scale, but there are others. *Matt Stone*

The look has held up well after 40 years, and the modernized interpretation is a handsome timepiece. McQueen's likeness has been used in several TAG Heuer advertisements. A limited *Le Mans*–edition Monaco was introduced in 2006, featuring orange and blue racing stripes on a black face with a Gulf Oil logo, commemorating the racing livery worn by those iconic Porsche 917s.

Ford went back to the McQueen/*Bullitt* well for another TV commercial used to introduce the 2005 Mustang. The plot is loosely based on the Kevin Costner film, *Field of Dreams*, and its iconic line, "Build it and they will come." In the Ford commercial, the protagonist carves a racetrack, instead of a baseball diamond, out of his cornfield. The Mustang used in the spot is painted silver, perhaps because the new car was not offered in Highland Green. The farmer pulls the Mustang out of his garage and up to the start/finish line of his newly built road course. Suddenly, a digitized McQueen, once again wearing

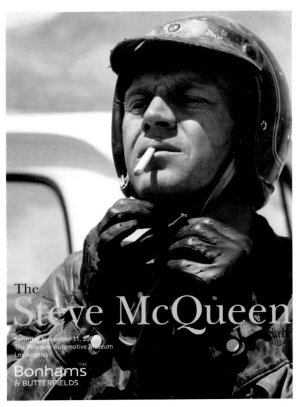

The catalog cover from the Steve McQueen auction held by Bonhams in Los Angeles, November 2006.

Left: Barbara Minty McQueen Brunsvold at the Bonhams auction, aboard one of her late husband's bikes that was sold at that event. She is a striking woman, remarried to David Brunsvold, and the couple are avid motorcycle enthusiasts. *Matt Stone* **Right:** Ford announced in September 2006 that it would build another Bullitt-edition for the 2008 model year. But *Motor Trend* magazine executed the idea even earlier, as evidenced by this 2005 Mustang GT wearing Bullitt-style wheels and the appropriate shade of Highland Green Metallic. This one-off, faux new Bullitt was built by Ford's West Coast public relations team in cooperation with *MT*'s editors for use in an article about the then-new Dodge Charger R/T (*MT*, July 2005). The Mustang was originally yellow and also had a rear wing, which was removed. The story celebrated *Bullitt*'s Chargers vs. Mustang theme, and Internet chat rooms were ablaze about a "Bullitt Mustang prototype spotted on a photo shoot in San Francisco." *Evan Klein*

the blazer and blue turtleneck made famous by Frank Bullitt, bolts out of the cornfield and heads straight for the car. There's an exchange of glances, and the astonished car owner flips McQueen the keys. Following the same theme as the Puma commercial, McQueen terrorizes the track, a tip of the hat to both the film and its star's driving prowess.

A second Steve McQueen memorabilia auction was held by Bonhams at the Petersen Automotive Museum on November 11, 2006. The first several hundred items sold were the property of Barbara Minty McQueen, including the 1958 GMC truck that McQueen used to drive around Beverly Hills, California. Other McQueen machines sold by a variety of owners were the Von Dutch Winton Flyer replica, the 1951 Hudson Wasp (both veterans of the 1984 sale), the Rolls-Royce Corniche Coupé used in the filming of 1968's *The Thomas Crown Affair*, the third of the first four Bullitt Mustangs, as well as several motorcycles.

Where can Steve McQueen's legacy go from here? There's no question he will remain one of the world's most popular actors and a still-relevant pop culture icon. He is revered in automotive, motorcy-cling, and motorsport circles. As a demonstration of his on-going popularity to car types, on September 15, 2006, Ford Motor Company Executive Vice President Mark Fields announced that the company will launch another Bullitt-edition Mustang for the 2008 model year.

The above-noted Ford Mustang commercial may have summarized it best. The spot contains no spoken dialog, ending simply with a font that reads, "The Legend Lives." Indeed.

INDEX

The McQueens at home in Brentwood, California, in 1968.
From foreground: Neile with her Excalibur, Steve with the XK-SS, Ferrari 275 GTS, Corvette, and a 1968 Mustang, possibly with some Shelby modifications. *Neile Adams collection*